MW01030183

THE GOOD, THE BAD, AND THE UGLY
NEW YORK RANGERS

THE GOOD, THE BAD, AND THE UGLY
NEW YORK RANGERS

HEART-POUNDING, JAW-DROPPING, AND GUT-WRENCHING
MOMENTS IN NEW YORK RANGERS HISTORY

Steve Zipay

TRIUMPH
BOOKS

Library of Congress Cataloging-in-Publication Data

Zipay, Steve, 1952–
    The good, the bad, and the ugly New York Rangers : heart-pounding, jaw-dropping, and gut-wrenching moments from New York Rangers history / Steve Zipay.
        p. cm.
    ISBN-13: 978-1-57243-965-8
    ISBN-10: 1-57243-965-3
    1. New York Rangers (Hockey team)—History. I. Title.

GV848.N43Z57 2008
796.962'64097471—dc22

                                                                2008035372

This book is available in quantity at special discounts for your group or organization. For further information, contact:

Triumph Books
542 South Dearborn Street
Suite 750
Chicago, Illinois 60605
(312) 939-3330
Fax (312) 663-3557

Printed in U.S.A.
ISBN-13: 978-1-57243-965-8
Design by Patricia Frey
Editorial and production by Prologue Publishing Services, LLC
All photos courtesy of AP Images unless otherwise indicated

CONTENTS

INTRODUCTION

Far better is it to dare mighty things, to win glorious triumphs even though checkered by failure, than to rank with those poor spirits who neither enjoy nor suffer much, because they live in the gray twilight that knows neither victory nor defeat.

—Theodore Roosevelt (1858–1919)

For more than 80 years, the players who have worn New York Rangers sweaters rarely traveled in Teddy's gray twilight. Instead, the Rangers, one of the NHL's Original Six teams, the one born amid the bright lights of Manhattan, certainly produced some shining moments, but more often succumbed to the sharp-angled shadows of defeat.

Still, what a ride.

Along the way, the Rangers have attracted hundreds of thousands of passionate, loyal followers—from firefighters to stockbrokers, from politicians to celebrities, from nurses to waitresses—a lineage that threads through families across the New York metropolitan area and beyond.

As a sportswriter and columnist, I was fortunate to be in Madison Square Garden during the spring of 1994, witnessing the magical run to the team's first Stanley Cup in 54 years. On the night that the Cup was raised, watching from the broadcast booth, I was awash with memories...

It was 1961.

My dad and uncles had already taken the youngsters in the family to Yankee Stadium and the Polo Grounds, but on this particular November night, I stood in a different kind of twilight, under the glorious marquee of the previous Garden on Eighth Avenue, about to enter for a game against the Chicago Blackhawks. Sure, we had watched games on television and hunkered down with the transistor radio. But this! Taxis honked, crowds buzzed, cigar smoke mingled with the scent of Nedick's hot dogs. Electricity. Bliss. That the Rangers won 4–1 was almost secondary.

Fast-forward to the late '60s and early '70s, hanging out in Section 420 of the current Garden, the blue seats, with former teammates from the Greenpoint Kings, our old roller-hockey team. When the Rangers weren't rocking the house, we'd venture into the Village to the old Fillmore East or back to the Garden for plenty of rock and roll in those years, as well.

Nineteen seventy-nine. An unexpected trip to the Finals against Montreal with an incredible group of players and characters: John Davidson, Anders Hedberg, Ulf Nilsson, Dave Maloney, Ron Greschner, Don Murdoch, Nick Fotiu, Walt Tkaczuk, Phil Esposito, Pat Hickey, Carol Vadnais...

The bitter years of falling short in the playoffs, while the upstart Islanders captured four straight championships in the early 1980s...

Then back to reality, there was Mark Messier, scoring epic goals, earning his place in New York sports lore, laughing and lifting the silver trophy in redemption.

Short-lived redemption, however.

After 1994 there were seasons of terrific individual performances from Wayne Gretzky, Brian Leetch, Adam Graves, Eric Lindros, and others that were eclipsed by failure. The Rangers didn't qualify for the playoffs from 1997–1998 to 2003–2004, the year before the NHL shut down in a dispute over—what else?—money.

When the dust settled, the Rangers, led by Czech superstar Jaromir Jagr, experienced a renaissance, making the postseason for three consecutive campaigns and reinvigorating the Garden.

Before the 2008–2009 season, the mercurial Jagr, his linemate Martin Straka, and the enigmatic agitator Sean Avery had gone their separate ways, clearing the stage for another cast. The club was fully in the hands of Swedish goaltender Henrik Lundqvist, centers Chris Drury and Scott Gomez, and an appealing group of homegrown prospects, the latter a rarity for the modern Rangers.

The book you hold isn't designed to be definitive or encyclopedic. The words won't resemble those of T.S. Eliot, who said, "History has many cunning passages, contrived corridors and issues." *The Good, the Bad, and the Ugly: New York Rangers* is anything but contrived.

Nor is it chronological. Think of it more as a jazz tune, the polyrhythms—sometimes sweet, sometimes discordant—of a longstanding professional sports franchise in New York: its owners, palaces, coaches, stars, role players, statistics, humor, heart, and soul. Which really ain't too bad.

ACKNOWLEDGMENTS

Thanks to my wife, Laura, and my daughter, Marisa, for love and encouragement; my parents, Steve and Lillian, who passed along their delight in sports, reading, and music; numerous friends and hockey colleagues, including Tim Clifford and Scott Cooper; luminaries such as Kenny Albert, John Davidson, Mike Emrick, Stan Fischler, Dave Maloney, Joe Micheletti, and Sam Rosen, as well as players and coaches who've shared stories and memories; all the newspapermen and women who've chronicled the team over the years; readers of—and contributors to—Blue Notes, my blog on newsday.com; and finally, my uncle, John N. Zipay, whose published dispatches and observations from New York, and wherever the U.S. Marine Corps sent him, certify him as the elder statesman of journalists in the family.

THE GOOD, THE BAD, AND THE UGLY
NEW YORK RANGERS

THE GOOD

J ust as baseball greatness is measured by World Series victories, having a team and its roster engraved on Lord Stanley's silver cup is the high point of an NHL franchise. Rangers names are etched four times on the sport's vaunted trophy, and the roads to the pinnacle are among the sweetest paths for this Original Six franchise, which has traveled hills and valleys over eight decades of competition.

1927–1928

The waning years of the 1920s were roaring for the Rangers.

In their inaugural 1926–1927 season, the Rangers finished an impressive 25–13–6. Right wing Bill Cook won the Art Ross Trophy with a league-high 33 goals, but the Rangers were ousted by the Boston Bruins in the opening round of the playoffs.

In their second campaign, the Rangers finished barely over .500 at 19–16–9, second in the American Division. But they advanced to the Finals by beating the Pittsburgh Pirates and the Boston Bruins, each in two games.

All the games in the best-of-five final series against the Montreal Maroons were scheduled for the Montreal Forum because the Ringling Brothers and Barnum & Bailey Circus—a major cash-cow spring event at Madison Square Garden—was booked.

1928 PLAYOFFS—GAME-BY-GAME RESULTS

Quarterfinals

March 27	Pittsburgh	4–0 W
March 29	Pittsburgh	2–4 L

Rangers defeat Pirates on total goals, 6–4

Semifinals

March 31	Boston	1–1 T
April 3	at Boston	4–1 W

Rangers advance to finals, topping Bruins on total goals, 5–2

Stanley Cup Finals

April 5	at Montreal	0–2 L
April 7	at Montreal	2–1 W (OT)
April 10	at Montreal	0–2 L
April 12	at Montreal	1–0 W
April 14	at Montreal	2–1 W

Rangers win Stanley Cup, beating the Maroons, 3 games to 2
Leading scorer: Frank Boucher, 7 goals, 1 assist (8 points)
Winning goal: Boucher, 3:35, 3rd period, Game 5

They were blanked 2–0 in the opener, but on April 7, the two teams played one of the most unforgettable games in hockey history.

The teams were scoreless halfway through the second period when Maroons forward Nels Stewart's shot struck Rangers netminder Lorne Chabot above the left eye. With no substitute, coach Lester Patrick—a 44-year-old former defenseman—donned the goaltending equipment.

Amazingly, Patrick held off the Maroons for the rest of the period, and in the third, Cook, the team's first captain, gave the Rangers a 1–0 lead. The Maroons scored to tie the game after two beautiful saves by Patrick, and sent the game into overtime—the first in Rangers history.

But Frank Boucher, the playmaking center on the Rangers' number-one line, stole the puck and scored the winner at 7:05 of

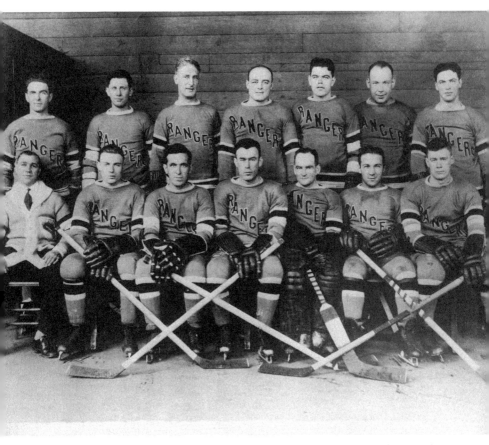

The New York Rangers sit for a team photo in New York on November 18, 1928. Starting on the top row, from left to right, are: Billy Boyd, Butch Keeling, manager Lester Patrick, Ching Johnson, Myles Lane, Taffy Abel, Paul Thompson. Bottom row: trainer Harry Westerby, Murray Murdock, Frank Boucher, Bill Cook, John Ross, Leo Bourgeault, Bun Cook.

the sudden-death session. The players lifted Patrick, who had been rebuffed when he first tried to "borrow" Alex Connell, an Ottawa Senators goalie who was watching from the stands, onto their shoulders and paraded around the rink.

The Rangers won two of the next three games, including the clincher on April 14, 1928, when Boucher again scored the deciding goal, and in their second season, the Rangers sipped from the silver bowl.

THE POEM

Twas in the spring of twenty-eight,
A golden Ranger page,
That Lester got a summons
To guard the Blueshirt cage.
Chabot had stopped a fast one,
A bad break for our lads,
The Cup at stake—and no one
To don the Ranger pads.
"We're cooked," lamented Patrick,
"This crisis I had feared."
He leaned upon his newest crutch
And wept inside his beard.
Then suddenly he came to life,
No longer halt or lame.
"Give me the pads," he bellowed,
"I used to play this game."
Then how the Rangers shouted,
How Patrick was acclaimed
Maroons stood sneering, gloating
They should have been ashamed.
The final score was two to one,
Old Lester met the test.
The Rangers finally won the Cup,
But Les has since confessed.
"I just spoke up to cheer the boys,
"I must have been delirious.
"But now in reminiscence,
"I'm glad they took me serious."
—James Burchard (November 1947)
New York World-Telegram

While the players returned to their homes in Canada, Patrick returned to New York and was given a hero's welcome, including a press conference on the steps of City Hall with media-savvy mayor Jimmy Walker, who had previously ordered a tickertape parade to celebrate Charles Lindbergh's transatlantic flight and posed with Babe Ruth after the Yankees slugger rapped his 60th homer.

In the public's eye, the Rangers were a glittering success.

1932–1933

For the five seasons following the 1928 Cup victory, the Rangers were contenders. They advanced to the Finals twice and the semis once before bowing out.

Boucher, the Cooks (Fred, or "Bun," and Bill, who was 37 and won his second Ross Trophy), and defenseman Ching Johnson formed the core of the club, which finished third in the American Division at 23–17–8. But other stars were showing their age, and some were shipped out. Goaltender Lorne Chabot was replaced by Glasgow-born Andy Aitkenhead, who played all 48

4

1933 PLAYOFFS—GAME-BY-GAME RESULTS

Quarterfinals
March 26   Montreal   5–2 W
March 28   at Montreal   3–3 T
Rangers top Canadiens on total goals, 8–5

Semifinals
March 30   Detroit   2–0 W
April 2   at Detroit   4–3 W
Rangers best Red Wings on total goals, 6–3

Stanley Cup Finals
April 4   Toronto   5–1 W
April 7   at Toronto   3–1 W
April 11   at Toronto   2–3 L
April 13   at Toronto   1–0 W (OT)
Rangers win second Stanley Cup, defeating the Maple Leafs, 3 games to 1
Leading scorer: Cecil Dillon, 8 goals, 2 assists (10 points)
Winning goal: Bill Cook, 7:34 OT, Game 4

games in the 1932–1933 season. Defenseman Earl Siebert replaced Taffy Abel.

In the playoffs, the Rangers first outlasted the Canadiens and then the Detroit Falcons, by virtue of total goals in each of the two-game series. Aitkenhead shut out the Falcons 2–0 in their first matchup.

Then it was on to Toronto to face the Maple Leafs and their high-scoring Kid Line of Charlie Conacher, Joe Primeau, and Busher Jackson in the best-of-five Finals.

The circus was on Broadway again, but at least the Rangers made the best of their one home game, beating the Leafs at the Garden 5–1 in Game 1 on April 4, with the so-called A-Line of Frank Boucher and the brothers Cook providing the offense. The next three games were in Toronto, with the Rangers ahead 2–0, the Leafs won the third game 3–2, but lost star Ace Bailey with torn cartilage in his knee.

Game 4, on April 13, 1933, turned out to be the clincher and another overtime thriller.

The teams were scoreless after three periods, with Aitkenhead continuing his brilliant play. In all, he allowed only 13 goals in eight games.

The decisive goal came after two Leafs—Alex Levinsky and Bill Thoms—were whistled for penalties, giving the Blueshirts a two-man advantage.

Bill Cook ended the contest after a pass from Butch Keeling at 7:34, and the win also drew the curtain on an era for the Rangers. The aging A-Line soon would be derailed with trades, and the team retooled under its new president, John Reed Kilpatrick.

The 1932–1933 trophy was known as the Forgotten Cup. Not only wasn't it formally presented to the team until November 11, 1933, the championship came between the more famous first and third Cups.

1939-1940

It began with the Powerhouse Line, continued with the Bread Line, and so on through the menu. This was probably the most complete and well-balanced club in Rangers history.

The main course, or the Powerhouse Line, was right wing Bryan Hextall, left wing Lynn Patrick (Lester's eldest son), and center Phillipe (Phil) Watson, who finished first, second, and third in league scoring, respectively.

The attempt to develop players in the team's farm system, begun by Patrick, was evident in the Bread Line of left wing Alex Shibicky (22) and brothers Neil (a center) and Mac Colville (a right wing).

With Mac only 20 and Neil just 22 when the trio was assembled in the 1936–1937 season, the threesome was the youngest in the league, and, according to reporters, was the "bread and butter" of the roster. And, remember, this was during the Depression, so over at St. Malachy's Roman Catholic Church a block away from the Garden, real bread lines were common.

Rounding out the feared offense was Wilfred "Dutch" Hiller, a left wing who was the fastest skater in the league; playmaking center Alf "the Embalmer" Pike; and right wing Clint "Snuffy" Smith, an elusive forward and faceoff specialist. Anchoring the defense was the captain, Art "the Trapper" Coulter, an outdoorsman, and goaltender Davey Kerr, who would win the Vezina Trophy. Kilby MacDonald, a spare forward, was named rookie of the year.

Although the team won just once in their first eight games (with three losses and four ties), it then caught fire. They were

Members of the Rangers pose with the Stanley Cup, which they won by defeating the Toronto Maple Leafs 3–2 in Toronto on April 13, 1940. Standing in the center is Rangers coach and manager Lester Patrick. In front of him is NHL president Frank Calder.

unbeaten in the next 17 games (14 wins and three ties). A 2–1 loss to Chicago finally snapped the string.

In the first round of the playoffs, the Rangers edged the second-best team, the Bruins, 4 games to 2, with Kerr posting 1–0 shutouts in Games 4 and 5.

The Maple Leafs were the final obstacle. The Rangers won the first two at the Garden, 2–1—when Pike beat goalkeeper Turk Broda at 15:30 of overtime—and 6–2. Because of the circus, the remainder of the Finals would be played in Toronto, and behind Broda, the Leafs took the next two games 2–1 and 3–0.

Muzz Patrick, who had scored only two goals in the 48-game regular season, ended Game 5 in overtime for a 2–1 win. In Game 6, the Leafs jumped out to a 2–0 lead, but third-period scores by Neil Colville and Pike knotted the game.

1940 PLAYOFFS—GAME-BY-GAME RESULTS

Semifinals

March 19	Boston	4–0 W
March 21	at Boston	2–4 L
March 24	at Boston	3–4 L
March 26	Boston	1–0 W
March 28	at Boston	1–0 W
March 30	Boston	4–1 W

Rangers take series, defeating Bruins 4 games to 2

Stanley Cup Finals

April 2	Toronto	2–1 W (OT)
April 3	Toronto	6–2 W
April 6	at Toronto	1–2 L
April 9	at Toronto	0–3 L
April 11	at Toronto	2–1 W (2OT)
April 13	at Toronto	3–2 W (OT)

Rangers win third Cup, outlasting Leafs, 4 games to 2
Leading Scorers (tie): Phil Watson, 3 goals, 6 assists (9 points);
Neil Colville, 2 points, 7 assists (9 points)
Winning Goal: Bryan Hextall Sr., 2:07 OT, Game 6

In overtime again, Hiller outmuscled a defenseman behind the net and flung a pass to Hextall at the blue line. Watson found Hextall, and, "It was kind of a fast play, bang-bang, just like that," Watson recalled years later. "Bryan came burning in like an elephant" and beat Broda with a high, hard backhander to the goalie's right. The team celebrated with champagne and the Cup in the Royal York Hotel in Toronto.

The players appreciated the talent and depth of the team, and Coulter said it could have been a dynasty had it not been for the circus, which forced them out of town—not only for games. Patrick took the team to Atlantic City for grueling workouts. "That alone cost us at least three Stanley Cups," said Coulter. "We won one, but we should have had four."

As it turned out, the next one would be 54 years away.

1993-1994

The drought seemed as if it would never end. The Rangers had climbed to the Finals in 1950, 1972, and 1979, but were denied the prize. So this run would be the most exhilarating and satisfying of all.

After finishing the regular season at the top of the NHL with 112 points, the Rangers met the Islanders, who only clinched a playoff berth in the next-to-last game of the season. Since 1975 the two archrivals had faced off in the postseason seven times, with Islanders winning five of those series.

Not this time.

The Rangers dominated and swept the series in four straight games, which included two back-to-back 6–0 shutouts at Madison Square Garden, and a total score of 22–3.

Following that rout, the Rangers knocked off the Washington Capitals to set up what would be two seven-game thrillers against the New Jersey Devils and the Vancouver Canucks.

In a spectacular series highlighted by captain Mark Messier's guarantee of a win prior to Game 6, the Devils took Game 1 in overtime, but goaltender Mike Richter blanked the Devils in Game 2. Stephane Matteau scored in double-overtime to cap Game 3. But

The indomitable Mark Messier led the Rangers to their first Stanley Cup in 54 years in 1994.

the Devils won Games 4 and 5, the latter by a commanding 4–1, and the Rangers were on the edge of the postseason abyss.

Then, taking a page from the great leaders in sports, Messier—who became even more of a mythic figure with his ensuing performance—audaciously promised a Game 6 victory in New Jersey to force a Game 7 at the Garden.

"We know we have to win it," he said. "We can win it, and we are going to win it."

Messier backed up his words in the most dramatic fashion possible. With the Devils ahead 2–0, the "Messiah" provided an assist and then scored three straight goals in the third period, the last into an empty net with 1:45 to play. "Game 6 was an incredible individual feat by Mark," Mike Keenan, the Rangers coach, said. "Historically, among the greatest ever."

It appeared that the Rangers would eliminate the Devils in regulation in Game 7, but Valeri Zelepukin scored with 7.7 seconds left to force overtime. The Rangers outshot the Devils 15–7 in the first extra stanza. Incredibly, at 4:24 of the second overtime, it was Matteau emerging the hero again, banging the puck off goalie Martin Brodeur's stick and in, ending a classic matchup.

Richter was outstanding in the finale as well, turning away the first 23 New Jersey shots and all eight in overtime. But the Pennsylvania netminder's best—and equally outstanding performances from Messier and Brian Leetch—was yet to come.

In the opener of the Finals in Vancouver, Leetch set up two goals, but the Canucks prevailed in overtime. After an empty-netter in the 3–1 victory in Game 3, Leetch scored twice in a 5–1 romp in Game 3.

It didn't stop there. In Game 4, with the Blueshirts trailing 2–0 in the first period, Leetch lit the lamp at 4:03 of the second period and added helpers on the next three Rangers goals for a four-point night and a 4–2 triumph.

Leetch's dominance notwithstanding, it was Richter's incredible split save, stopping a penalty shot by "the Russian Rocket," Pavel Bure, with his right skate at 6:31 of the second period, that kept the game in reach.

With the Rangers ahead in the series 3–1, the Garden faithful were sky-high for Game 5, chanting, "We want the Cup," but were silenced by a 6–3 Vancouver win. The Canucks won again to tie the series in Canada, and on June 14, all of New York and the hockey world was watching.

Leetch beat Canucks goaltender Kirk McLean for a 1–0 lead in the first period, and Messier potted a rebound in the second to extend the margin to 3–1. The Rangers held on to win 3–2, sparking a joyous celebration that the Garden had never witnessed—and hasn't since.

"Bure and MacTavish with one and six-tenths seconds to go," longtime Rangers voice Marv Albert reported from the radio booth. "The puck is dropped. MacTavish controls, and it's all over! The New York Rangers have won the Stanley Cup...something that most people thought they would never hear in their lifetime. And the Rangers pour onto the ice to pound each other. Mike Richter being congratulated. And they are going wild at Madison Square Garden!"

Said Rod Gilbert, the former Rangers right wing who was pounding the Plexiglas in glee: "I lost my voice in both French and English."

Leetch was named MVP, and the demons of a painful half-century had been vanquished. As the players skated around with the Cup, one middle-aged fan underscored the relief of a generation of fans with a sign.

It read: "Now I Can Die in Peace."

THE NEAR MISSES

In hockey, the ultimate success, the culmination of many a boyhood dream, is hoisting the Stanley Cup. The Rangers often had high-quality teams that just fell slightly short. Here are the stories of three near-misses.

1949–1950
Coached by Lynn Patrick, this group of Rangers scored the fewest goals in the six-team circuit, but finished fourth in the regular

1994 PLAYOFFS—GAME-BY-GAME RESULTS

Eastern Conference Quarterfinals

April 17	Islanders	6–0	W
April 18	Islanders	6–0	W
April 21	at Islanders	5–1	W
April 24	at Islanders	5–2	W

Rangers sweep rival Islanders, 4 games to 0

Eastern Conference Semifinals

May 1	Washington	6–3	W
May 3	Washington	5–2	W
May 5	at Washington	3–0	W
May 7	at Washington	2–4	L
May 9	Washington	4–3	W

Rangers oust Capitals, 4 games to 1

Eastern Conference Finals

May 15	New Jersey	3–4	L (2 OT)
May 17	New Jersey	4–0	W
May 19	at New Jersey	3–2	W (2 OT)
May 21	at New Jersey	1–3	L
May 23	New Jersey	1–4	L
May 25	at New Jersey	4–2	W
May 27	New Jersey	2–1	W (2 OT)

Rangers edge Devils, 4 games to 3

Stanley Cup Finals

May 31	Vancouver	2–3	L (OT)
June 2	Vancouver	3–1	W
June 4	at Vancouver	5–1	W
June 7	at Vancouver	4–2	W
June 9	Vancouver	3–6	L
June 11	at Vancouver	1–4	L
June 14	Vancouver	3–2	W

Rangers win fourth Cup, beating Canucks 4 games to 3

Leading Scorer: Brian Leetch, 11 goals, 23 assists (34 points)

Winning Goal: Mark Messier, 13:29, second period, Game 7

TOP 5 TRADES

1. When you can get a player who can transform a franchise, almost no price is too high. On October 4, 1991, the Rangers acquired the legendary Mark Messier from the Edmonton Oilers for Bernie Nicholls, Steven Rice, and Louis DeBrusk. Quite a steal. Three years later, the popular, gritty captain—soon to be dubbed "the Messiah"—skated joyously around the Garden, hoisting the franchise's first Stanley Cup in 54 years.

2. February 22, 1964. This multiplayer, star-laden blockbuster was the biggest in Rangers history at the time: Bob Nevin and Dick Duff, defenseman Arnie Brown, Rod Seiling and Billy Collins came from Toronto for Andy Bathgate and smooth-as-silk center Don McKenney. Bathgate was a Rangers legend, but Nevin wore the captain's C from 1965 to 1971, and Brown and Seiling were the guts of the revamped team assembled by general manager Emile Francis. Duff was soon dealt to the Montreal Canadiens for Billy Hicke.

3. August 19, 1947. Maybe the Canadiens thought Buddy O'Connor was too old at 31. They were wrong. When O'Connor, who had been a member of two Cup winners in Montreal, was dealt to the Rangers, the fans of the bleu, blanc, et rouge were surprised. O'Connor arrived with Frank Eddolls for Joe Bell, Hal Laycoe, and George Robertson, and in his first season with the Blueshirts, he recorded career-highs in goals, with 24, and points, with 60. The Rangers made the playoffs, and he fell short of the league scoring title by only one point. Nonetheless, he won the Hart Trophy as the league's MVP as well as the Lady Byng Trophy, given to the most gentlemanly player. He was the first player to win both awards in the same season, and he was named Canada's athlete of the year for 1948. He was inducted into the Hall of Fame in 1988.

4. June 4, 1963. Gump Worsley, Dave Balon, Len Ronson, and Leon Rochefort were shipped to the Canadiens for Jacques Plante, Donnie Marshall, and Phil Goyette. Yes, Worsley went on to win Stanley Cups with Montreal, and perennial All-Star Plante pouted and played only two subpar years in New York. But Goyette and Marshall flourished, and Balon, a minor-league hopeful at the time, returned in a trade with Minnesota in 1968 and the left wing twice led the Rangers in goals. Goyette, in the next six seasons, netted 97 goals and dished out 227

assists. Marshall, who had terrific defensive skills, blossomed offensively in his seven seasons. In 1965–1966, he had 26 goals and 28 assists. Ronson and Rochefort were throw-ins.

5. October 2, 1981. Slick center Mike Rogers (and a 10th-round pick) arrived from Hartford in exchange for Chris Kotsopoulos, Gerry McDonald, and Doug Sulliman. From 1981 to 1986, Rogers played 316 games, scored 117 goals, and contributed 191 assists for almost a point-a-game average. He became only the third player—Jean Ratelle and Vic Hadfield preceded him—to score 100 points in a season, with 38 goals and 65 assists. And he became only the third player in NHL history at the time to score 100 points in his first three NHL seasons. He had good company: Wayne Gretzky and Peter Stastny. (Mario Lemieux later joined the club.) His 16-game point streak in February and March 1982 was a team record for nearly 10 years until it was surpassed by Brian Leetch in 1991–1992.

season, thanks to the play of goaltender Chuck Rayner, who teammates called "the Lone Ranger."

In the first round of the playoffs, the Rangers upset Montreal 4–1, helped by five goals from Pentti Lund, a Finnish forward who had won the Calder Trophy. The Ringling Brothers circus was again booked at Madison Square Garden in April, and the Rangers were evicted for the Finals. The Rangers chose to play two "home" games against the Detroit Red Wings at Maple Leaf Gardens in Toronto.

At the Olympia in Detroit, the Wings—playing without their injured star Gordie Howe—captured Game 1, 4–1. In Toronto, the teams split, but the Rangers took Games 4 and 5 on overtime goals by Don Raleigh. "They seemed like a team of destiny," said Max McNab, a Red Wings center.

It certainly looked that way when the Rangers led 3–1 early in the second period in Game 6 and 4–3 early in the third. But the desperate Detroit Red Wings tied it on Ted Lindsay's goal at 4:13, and won it on a goal by Sid Abel at 10:34. In the decisive Game 7, on goals by Allan Stanley and Tony Leswick, the Blueshirts led 2–0, but the teams were tied 3–3 after two periods, then three, and even after the first overtime.

A utility forward by the name of Pete Babando won the Cup for Detroit. George Gee won a faceoff from Buddy O'Connor in the circle to Rayner's right and drew the puck to Babando at the top of the circle. Babando's shot hit a player, changed direction, and zipped past Rayner into the far corner of the net. "I didn't see it until it was coming right through, about two inches off the ice," said Rayner.

Said Raleigh: "In sports, you win or you don't. Nobody remembers how close you come."

Well, Rayner remembered. "Not a day goes by that I don't think about that goal," Rayner said a long time later, reflecting on the loss. "What a shame that was. Just one goal, and there never would have been a 54-year drought."

1971–1972

Under coach Emile "the Cat" Francis, the Rangers made the playoffs from the 1966–1967 season through the next nine years. The 1971–1972 squad was the cream of the crop.

Rod Gilbert, the right wing who broke in with the Rangers in 1960, had 43 goals and 54 assists that season and proclaimed it "our best team."

With Gilbert's G-A-G (Goal-a-Game) Line leading the way, the club ended the season at a terrific 48–17–13. And with Gilbert, left wing Vic Hadfield (50 goals, 56 assists), center Jean Ratelle (46–63), defenseman Brad Park, and goaltender Ed Giacomin starring, the team was poised for their first Cup since 1940.

Things were rolling along until Ratelle was struck by a Dale Rolfe shot that fractured his ankle with 17 games left in the regular season. Although Ratelle was not the same swift playmaker in the postseason, the Rangers edged Montreal in the first round and swept the Blackhawks in four games.

In the Finals, the Rangers gave it a yeoman's effort against the Bruins, who were vying for their second Cup in three years. But Hall of Fame defenseman–to-be Bobby Orr and the formidable line of Phil Esposito, Ken Hodge, and Wayne Cashman (all of whom would join the Rangers later in their careers) were too much, and the B's special teams stifled the G-A-G Line.

"They had Derek Sanderson and Eddie Westfall killing penalties. Don Marcotte checked the hell out of me," Gilbert said.

And goaltender Gerry Cheevers made a stand at the end.

Opening the series in noisy Boston Garden, the Beantowners won the first two games 6–5 and 2–1.

At Madison Square Garden, the Rangers split Games 3 and 4, but won 3–2 in Game 5 in Boston. The Rangers took Game 6 to force a seventh and deciding match.

In Game 7, Orr scored in the first period, Cashman added two more, and Cheevers was unbeatable. "They're not going to get a pea by me," he reportedly had told Cashman. The Rangers didn't put any vegetables, or pucks, in the cage, and another opportunity to end the curse of 1940 went by the boards.

1978–1979

Freddie the Fog. Ooh-la-la-Sasson commercials. A player suspended for cocaine possession. A Denis Potvin check that essentially ended Ulf Nilsson's season and begat a vulgar chant that lasts to this day.

The 1978–1979 Rangers season had all that and more—overachievers who skated to the Stanley Cup Finals but were driven out unceremoniously. The culprits? Some partying, an injured goaltender, and a little twist of fate.

In their first season under the enigmatic coach Fred Shero, nicknamed "the Fog" for often drifting into his own world, the Rangers were a diverse bunch: two Swedish free agents, Nilsson and Anders Hedberg, who scored 60 goals between them; veteran captain Phil Esposito, the former Bruin, who scored 42 by himself; Don Murdoch, suspended for 40 games after Toronto customs found more than 4 grams of coke in a sock; mop-topped Ron Duguay of the Sasson jeans commercials; Staten Island–born enforcer Nick Fotiu; cigar-smoking dandy Carol Vadnais; brothers Don and Dave Maloney; and solid citizens Walt Tkaczuk and Steve Vickers.

Chemistry carried them past the Kings in the first round. They beat the Flyers in five and the hated Islanders in six. "The battle with the Islanders took a lot out of the team," recalled Nilsson,

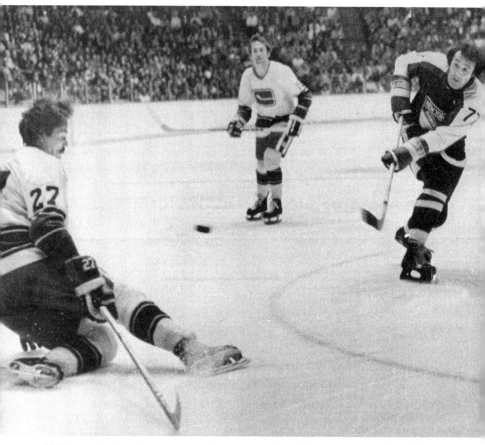

Phil Esposito fires the puck past defenseman Harold Snepsts to net his 600th NHL goal on November 4, 1977. Photo courtesy of Getty Images.

whose ankle was broken on a Potvin check on February 25 and missed all but two playoff games.

The Finals opponent was the deep Canadiens, who had won three straight Cups with vets Guy Lafleur, Steve Shutt, Jacques Lemaire, Yvan Cournoyer, Bob Gainey, Larry Robinson, and Serge Savard.

Still, the Rangers won Game 1, and Esposito, wary of the upcoming celebration, suggested that the team move to a Montreal suburb to get away from the nightlife. Shero declined. "I think you're making a mistake," Espo said he told the coach.

According to Esposito, several Rangers partied all night and were in no shape to give their all.

Before that second game, fate may have intervened as well. Canadiens coach Scotty Bowman was going to replace goalie Ken Dryden with Bunny Larocque, but in warmups, Larocque was shaken by a shot that struck his mask. Dryden was back in, allowed two goals early, but only five more after that in the series. Esposito said, "We just died. We stopped. We went in reverse. We took a 2–0 lead in the second game and never won another faceoff."

In the other cage was John Davidson, playing in severe pain after injuring his left knee against the Islanders, and he couldn't hold the fort. The Canadiens swept the next four, 6–2, 4–1, 4–3, and 4–1, and Davidson had major knee surgery afterward.

Another memorable season, but with no finishing kick.

IN THE RAFTERS

Rod Gilbert

His No. 7 was the first to be raised to the roof on October 14, 1979.

Gilbert, a right wing, was born in Montreal in 1941 and first came to the Rangers on a one-game call-up on November 27, 1960, and recorded an assist. He was a Ranger for good in 1962 and played 1,065 games—the third-highest in franchise history. From 1960 to 1977, he scored 406 goals and added 615 assists. An eight-time All-Star, Gilbert's finest season was 1971–1972, when he tallied 43 goals and 54 assists as part of the G-A-G (Goal-a-Game) Line with Jean Ratelle and Vic Hadfield, who finished 3, 4, and 5 in the league scoring race that season. Gilbert was inducted into the NHL Hall of Fame in 1982.

Ed Giacomin

On March 5, 1989, the goaltender's No. 1 jersey was the second to be retired.

During his 10-year career, the Garden often resounded with the cheer "Ed-die, Ed-die," and why not? Giacomin, originally from Sudbury, Ontario, holds the franchise record for shutouts with 49, and his 267 victories in 539 games ranks second all-time. Giacomin, who was inducted into the Hall of Fame in 1987, shared the league's top goaltending honor—the Vezina Trophy—with Gilles Villemure in 1971. But at 36, he was waived and claimed by Detroit. Three days later, on November 2, 1975, when he returned to the Garden as a Red Wing, the house rocked and chanted his name as a tribute to his years on Broadway. Giacomin wept in the crease behind his mask, raised his stick to calm the applause, and the Red Wings won 6–4.

Mike Richter
His No. 35 jersey was put on display on February 4, 2004.

Richter, one of the club's most popular players in the '90s, backstopped the team in its 1993–1994 Stanley Cup championship season. During that Cup run, he established records for playoff wins (16) and shutouts (four). A three-time U.S. Olympian, Richter spent his entire career (1989–2003) with the Blueshirts. A second-round draft pick in 1985, the Abington, Pennsylvania, native ended up playing 666 games between the pipes and winning 301 games, both franchise records. His stellar goals-against percentage of 2.89 and his .904 save percentage pay tribute to his distinction as the franchise's best goaltender, and the only one who later attended Yale.

Mark Messier
The fourth honoree, his No. 11 was retired on January 12, 2006.

While the Rangers are famous for nicknames, there will forever be only one "Captain," and that is the incredible Messier, who put an exclamation point on his legendary career by leading the team to the Stanley Cup for the first time in 54 years in 1994. The Edmonton native, who first came to the Rangers in 1991 after winning five Cups with the Oilers, immediately led the team in scoring with 107 points and won his second Hart Trophy as league MVP. His impressive array of stats compiled over a 16-year career—he left the sport second on the league's all-time scoring list with 1,887 points—doesn't reflect his true value as a gritty,

NHL Hall of Famer Rod Gilbert played 1,065 games with the Rangers and scored 1,021 points in 18 seasons. Photo courtesy of Getty Images.

take-no-prisoners leader whose exploits in that memorable 1993–1994 Stanley Cup playoff run are the stuff of legend.

Brian Leetch

His No. 2 was retired on January 24, 2008. The former captain—considered by many to be the greatest American defenseman to play in the NHL—holds the Rangers' records of 741 assists, as well as 240 goals by a defenseman, and ranks second in team history with 981 points and 1,129 games. Born in Texas, Leetch grew up in the northeast and attended Boston College. The Rangers' first-round pick (ninth overall) in 1986, he won the Calder Trophy as rookie of the year in 1988–1989 when he scored 23 goals and 71 points. He won the Norris Trophy twice, in 1992 and 1997, and in between, in 1994, when the Rangers won the Stanley Cup, he was awarded the Conn Smythe Trophy as playoff MVP, the only American to ever win the award.

Adam Graves

In 2009 a sixth jersey was to be retired, the No. 9 worn by the popular Graves, who played in New York from 1991–1992 to 2000–2001. Graves, whose statistics aren't the only measure of the man, scored 52 goals in the 1993–1994 Stanley Cup Championship season and had also won a Cup in Edmonton. Many fans believe that Andy Bathgate, who also wore No. 9 for much of his Rangers career, which began in 1952 and ended in 1964, should share the honor.

THE BAD

Seems like every pro sports franchise has its superstitions and jinxes. The hapless Red Sox vanquished "the Curse of the Bambino" when they beat the Yankees in the ALCS and won the World Series for the first time since 1918 in 2004.

The Rangers just may have been victimized by their own curse, which supposedly bedeviled the franchise for 54 years.

The hex involves the year 1940, the third time the franchise had won the Stanley Cup, and there are two versions of the origins of the curse. One or perhaps both—triggered the derisive "19-40" taunt that resonated through the homes of the rival Islanders and Devils during tight playoffs series a half-century later.

ANGERING THE HOCKEY GODS

During the 1940–1941 season, the one following the Cup-clinching, the mortgage on the 15-year-old Madison Square Garden was paid off, and in a public display of glee, management burned the document in the bowl of the prestigious silver trophy.

According to some Canadian fans who held the Cup in almost spiritual esteem, the hockey gods cursed the Rangers for this desecration of the Holy Grail of the sport.

A more complex explanation stems from another rival team—and Madison Square Garden co-tenant—the New York Americans, who were the first NHL team in New York, born in the 1925–1926 season, when the Garden first opened its doors.

Once the Madison Square Garden Corporation saw that hockey would be successful, the Rangers were founded, and the Americans—or Amerks—foundered without the corporation's financial support. The NHL assumed ownership of the Amerks in 1937, and they beat the Rangers in the playoffs in 1938, but lost to the Chicago Blackhawks in the semifinals.

With the coming of World War II, the Americans lost almost all their players to the armed forces, and the league folded the franchise after the 1941 season.

Amerks owner Red Dutton blamed Rangers management for encouraging league officials to kill the New York competitor, and as compensation, Dutton was named league president in 1943.

Rules weren't changed to punish the Rangers, but Dutton vowed that the Rangers would never win the Cup for as long as he lived. When he died at age 88—in 1987—it had been 47 years since the glorious Cup victory of 1940.

BLAME IT ON THE CURSES

Maybe the curses were bunk, but some strange misfortunes derailed the Rangers' Cup hopes in the ensuing years. In fact, they hardly made the playoffs in 1950s and '60s, and in 1972 advanced to the Cup Finals but fell to the Boston Bruins.

Did the curse play a role?

Well, some thought so. Jean Ratelle, the Rangers, lithe, gifted center, broke his right ankle 17 games before the end of the 1971–1972 season. "That injury probably cost us the Stanley Cup," coach Emile Francis said after Boston captured the Finals in six games. "With Jean, we were right there," Francis lamented. "Without him, [Bobby] Orr took control, and the Bruins won. It was a shame."

The following season, the Rangers finally had their first local competitor since the Amerks: the upstart, expansion Islanders, who earned a playoff berth two years later and knocked out the Rangers. The Rangers returned the favor four years later but couldn't secure the Cup, losing to the Montreal Canadiens in the Finals.

The "19-40" chant began soon after, when the Islanders made an incredible run of winning four straight Cups, beginning in 1980, surpassing the Rangers' total of three.

Most observers point to the 1984 semifinal playoff series—won by the Isles in overtime of the fifth game against the Rangers—as when the chant really became a staple for anti-Rangers fans.

In 1992 and 1993, some believe the curse of 1940 struck again.

The Rangers stormed to the best overall record in the NHL and met the Devils in the division semifinals, when the "19-40" chant migrated to New Jersey. The Rangers prevailed, but fell to the defending champion Pittsburgh Penguins in the Patrick Division Finals in 1992. During one game, a long, long shot by Penguins center Ron Francis uncharacteristically skipped past Rangers net-minder Mike Richter.

In 1993 the Rangers finished last, thanks in part to an odd incident. Star defenseman Brian Leetch, getting out of a taxi outside of the Garden, slipped—on some ice, ironically—and shattered his ankle.

The next season, the Devils squared off with the Rangers again—this time in the division semifinals, and New Jersey led the best-of-seven series 3–2, with the sixth game scheduled at Brendan Byrne Arena, where much was made of the fact that the seating capacity was 19,040. Curse or coincidence?

With the Rangers facing elimination, steely-eyed captain Mark Messier stepped into the role of myth-buster. He guaranteed that his club would push the series to a seventh and deciding game. "We know we're going to go in there and win Game 6 and bring it back to the Garden," Messier declared.

For some, the curse's hold seemed to be strong, as the Devils had a 2–1 lead in the third period, but Messier scored three straight goals for a 4–2 win.

Back at the Garden for Game 7 and leading 1–0, with the series all but wrapped up, another stunner occurred: the Devils' Valeri Zelepukin scored with a scant 7.7 seconds left in regulation to force overtime. But Stephane Matteau scored in the second overtime to vault the Rangers into the Finals, where Messier finally buried the whammy with the winning goal in Game 7 against the Vancouver Canucks.

Even play-by-play man Sam Rosen referred to the vanquishing of the storied hex in his final remarks from the television booth at the delirious Garden as the final seconds ticked off: "That's it! Fifty-four years of curses are over! No more 1940! The New York Rangers are the Stanley Cup champions! And this one will last a lifetime! Let the celebration begin!"

THE WORST TRADES

Trades can bring a team valuable assets. Trades can also haunt a franchise for decades. Some trades work out for each club, either in the short term or the long run. The Rangers have had plenty of each.

No. 1—Hands down, not only the most disastrous trade in Rangers history, but one of the most lopsided transactions in NHL history, was the swap of Rick Middleton to Boston for the veteran Ken Hodge on May 26, 1976.

The exchange of right wings was made because Rangers center Phil Esposito badly wanted to play with the veteran Hodge, his former linemate in Beantown, and he persuaded general manager John Ferguson to ship the 22-year-old Middleton—who had scored 22 and 24 goals in his first two seasons as a Ranger—north.

Oh, my.

Middleton starred in Boston for 12 years, compiling five straight seasons of at least 40 goals and 90 points, and amassed 402 goals and almost 900 points in the Hub. He was a three-time All-Star and won the Lady Byng Trophy.

Meanwhile, Hodge, one of the few NHL players to be born in England (Birmingham), had been an offensive force when he played with Esposito.

In New York, he was a bust. He scored 23 goals in a little more than a season in New York before he was sent down to the Rangers' farm club, the New Haven Nighthawks, and retired.

"Why, oh why, did I ever trade Rick Middleton?" Ferguson moaned years later.

No. 2—In some ways, this November 7, 1975, deal with the Bruins set the table for number one (Middleton).

Defenseman Brad Park and graceful, playmaking center Jean Ratelle, along with a guy who later became a trivia answer, Joe Zanussi, were swapped for Esposito and defenseman Carol Vadnais.

Ratelle, who had played for the Rangers for 15 years and had been the pivot for the G-A-G (Goal-a-Game) Line with Rod Gilbert and Vic Hadfield, scored 155 goals and added 295 assists in the next six seasons for Boston. He retired in 1981 and was elected to the Hall of Fame four years later.

> **"I BELIEVE FUNDAMENTALLY WE ARE THE WORST TEAM IN THE NATIONAL HOCKEY LEAGUE."**
> —BOBBY HOLIK, AFTER A 9–1 LOSS TO OTTAWA IN JANUARY 2004

Park, the first Rangers draft pick to ever play for the club, led the team with 25 goals and 57 assists for 82 points in 1973–1974. The 25 goals remain the record for a Rangers defenseman, and he was named captain in 1974–1975.

"I had no inkling at all of such a trade, and from what I understand, neither did Ratelle or Espo," Park said later. As it turned out, the Bruins were looking for someone to replace the legendary Bobby Orr, whose knee injuries were about to force him into retirement. "All the so-called knowledgeable hockey people were saying New York got the best of the deal, and I had to go out and show Boston fans that they got the best of it," he recalled.

That's what Park did. The Bruins were a champion with him.

Esposito led the Rangers in scoring for the next few years and led the Rangers to the Cup Finals in 1979, but he never came close to his Boston scoring stats. The long-term damage was done. Later, as Rangers general manager for three years in the mid-1980s, he was saddled with the nickname "Trader Phil" for acquiring the aging Marcel Dionne and surrendering a first-round pick as compensation for signing the fading Michel Bergeron. But he did draft defenseman Brian Leetch, who would break virtually all of Park's records as a Ranger.

Vadnais, who received $100,000 to waive his no-trade clause, was a solid defenseman who scored 20 goals for the Rangers that season and played six more on Broadway. But fans who considered the trade of the popular duo an insult never warmed to Vadnais. One of the regular serenades was: "Hit 'em with your purse, Carol."

No. 3—This one completed the hat trick.

On January 1, 1987, with Esposito as general manger, the Rangers sent two players who energized the Garden with their hustle—center Mike Ridley and right wing Kelly Miller—to Washington for Bobby Carpenter, a former 50-goal scorer. Yikes.

Carpenter played in just 28 games, scoring two goals in 1986–1987, and was traded to Los Angeles. Ridley played seven seasons for the Caps, scoring from 23 to 41 goals in every one. Miller finished his career in D.C., ending with 1,057 games under this belt.

To use the term *lopsided* doesn't do justice to the word.

No. 4—To Rangers fans, March 2, 2004, is a date which lives in infamy. After 17 years on Broadway, as part of a sweeping salary dump/roster-cleansing, general manager Glen Sather traded Brian Leetch, their franchise's greatest defenseman and one of its most popular players, to the Maple Leafs for two 21-year-old prospects (defenseman Maxim Kondratiev and forward Jarkko Immonen, who didn't pan out) and two draft choices.

Leetch probably could have been ushered out more gracefully and allowed to retire as a Ranger or even play another year. But the $6.5 million owed him was too much for the Rangers, who were on the verge of missing the playoffs for the seventh consecutive season. Instead, he played solidly for Toronto and then Boston, and some fans in 2006–2007 were still clamoring for a return.

What left Leetch—and fans—bitter was the way he was dispatched, on his 36th birthday. But Leetch remained semi-retired, enjoying family life in Boston, and has said the only place he would have returned to was New York, where he still has family ties. His No. 2 was retired on January 24, 2008, without the Rangers ever finding a suitable replacement.

Nos. 5 & 6—These next two, while not of the magnitude of the others, deserve to be included.

March 19, 1993. Doug Weight to the Oilers for Esa Tikkanen.

Sure, Tikkanen was a valued role player in the drive to the Cup the following season.

But Weight led the Oilers for the next eight years, then was a solid vet for the Blues, and, when traded to the Carolina Hurricanes in 2006, helped them win the Cup.

August 31, 1995. Defenseman Sergei Zubov and center Petr Nedved went to Pittsburgh for center Luc Robitaille and defenseman Ulf Samuelsson. Argggh. The talent scale tipped the other way.

Twelve years later, the Rangers' power play has never been the same as it was with Leetch and Zubov. In fact, the Russian blueliner is still putting up terrific numbers with Dallas and just might be a Hall of Fame candidate. Nedved has pretty much run out of road, but he posted some very good numbers with the Penguins.

Robitaille was at the tail end of his career with the Rangers. Samuelsson was slower and older than Zubov.

MISSPENT MILLIONS: THE FREE-AGENT BUSTS

July has been one of the cruelest months for the Rangers. It is the NHL's free-agent season, and over the years, the Rangers have doled out tens of millions of dollars on underachievers in the twilight of their careers.

Here's some of the more infamous, the Dirty Dozen:

Zdeno Ciger

Signed in July 2001, the aging left wing played 29 games. He scored six goals, had seven assists, and was traded five months later to Tampa for Matthew Barnaby. Z, we hardly knew ye.

Igor Ulanov

The hulking 6'3" Russian defenseman was another July 2001 disaster. He was dispatched—with Filip Novak and a pair of first- and fourth-round picks for Pavel Bure—in March 2002 after 39 games in which he contributed a whopping six assists and didn't hit with the intensity advertised. Some say he was a cheap-shot artist rather than a true enforcer.

Dave Karpa

Yet another July 2001 acquisition, Karpa had played 11 nondescript years in the NHL before coming to New York. The brawling, oft-injured defenseman from Saskatchewan appeared in 94 games, logged 145 minutes in the sin bin, contributed one goal and 12 assists, was released, and ended up in Russia, skating for Khabarovsk Amur.

Scott Fraser

In 1997 the right wing earned about $310,000 from the Edmonton Oilers. But the Rangers opened the wallet for him in 1998, delivering a three-year contract worth about $4 million. The result: 28 games, two goals, four assists, and a demotion to the minors. Fraser then retired from hockey.

Valeri Kamensky

In 1999 the 33-year-old forward, a star and gold medalist in Russia who won a Stanley Cup with Colorado in his seven-year NHL career, signed for five years at $21 million. Kamensky, a good guy, was on the downslide, however. He wound up being a high-maintenance player with low stats (27 goals and 39 assists in 123 games) in New York. After being sent to Dallas in 2001–2002, he left the NHL after finishing the season in New Jersey.

Sylvain Lefebvre

Another Cup winner in Colorado (he had his daughter, Alexzandra, baptized in the silver trophy after the 1996 season), the 31-year-old defenseman was given $10 million for four years with a fifth-year option for another $3 million. Naturally, once he landed in New York, his career cratered. In three and a half seasons, he produced four, count 'em, four goals and 30 assists. In 2002–2003 he was assigned to the minors, then played in Switzerland and retired.

Theo Fleury

Beset by psychological problems, the little dynamo was a $28 million, four-year headache. Actually, he only lasted three and left behind a trail of temper tantrums, obscene gestures to fans, suspensions, and rehabs for alcohol and substance abuse. When he was in his prime, Fleury was dynamite. In New York, he mostly imploded.

Bruce Driver

After 11 good seasons in New Jersey—including the Devils' championship year in 1995—it was decided by the brain trust that the 33-year-old veteran would be a fine fit in 1996. Wrong. In three subpar years (13 goals in 210 games), Driver didn't earn his $3.9 million. And compounding the error, he could not be dealt. Driver was among the first wave of NHL players to sign a contract with a no-trade clause.

Stephane Quintal

After playing parts of 12 seasons in the NHL, the Rangers took a flyer on the 30-year-old defenseman in 1999, giving him a pact worth $14 million over five years. Forget flying; Quintal crashed, with two goals and 14 assists in 75 games. He was put on waivers in October 2000 and claimed by the Blackhawks. In 2005 he told Montreal's *La Presse* that he used stimulants on a regular basis and believed about 40 percent of the players he'd encountered took stimulants and that some used anabolic steroids.

Vladimir Malakhov

A torn ACL that sidelined Malakhov for much of the previous season didn't stop GM Glen Sather from signing the 31-year-old defenseman to a four-year, $14 million contract in July 2000. At the time, he became only the third player to skate with each of the New York area teams. He was drafted by the Islanders and was traded to the Devils. As a Ranger, Malakhov played 211 games and had 12 goals, 53 assists, and 192 penalty minutes. Nothing to write home about. He was traded in the March 2004 purge to Philadelphia for Rick Kozak and a second-round draft choice.

Theo Fleury spent much of his time as a Ranger down in the dumps.

Greg DeVries

For a 30-year-old fellow who never scored more than 20 points in a season until the 2002–2003 campaign, defenseman DeVries was handsomely rewarded by the Rangers: four years, $14 million in July 2003. By March 2004, when the Rangers began a major salary dump, he was in Ottawa, swapped for Karel Rachunek and Alexandre Giroux.

Steve McKenna
Outside of sheer size—the largest Ranger ever at 6'8", 255 pounds—McKenna brought little to the table. A poor skater, McKenna spent most of his time in New York in 2002 in the penalty box: 18 fighting majors in 54 games. Last we heard, he was coaching hockey in a place where most of the ice is in cocktails: Australia.

THE WORST DRAFTS

Drafting teenage players is, at best, an inexact science.

Scouts who dutifully trek to games from the hinterlands of Canada to the rinks of Europe provide the information and, in modern times, the video.

But in many cases, especially after the first round, when there is usually some general agreement on the potential of these youngsters, it's a roll of the dice.

Successful franchises hit the mark on their top picks, allowing their farm systems to fill gaps in the big club's roster in case of injuries or trades.

Here are some of the Rangers' most dubious choices, the ones that, for various reasons—even though they were considered solid picks—just didn't pan out. Their failures to develop and succeed in the NHL were costly and kept the franchise in the doldrums for decades, forcing the signings of free agents in an attempt to be competitive.

Pavel Brendl
Not just one of the biggest busts in Rangers draft history, the Czech forward ranks as one of the most disappointing selections in the annals of the league. After a 1999 draft-day swap of Niklas Sundstrom, Dan Cloutier, and a third-rounder to the Tampa Bay Lightning for the number-four pick, Brendl was chosen. And why not?

He led the Western Hockey League in goals with 73 in 68 games and was the Canadian major junior hockey rookie of the year. But his indifferent attitude and preparation infuriated the

Pavel Brendl, shown here with an apple after being acquired by the Rangers in 1999, is one of the biggest busts in Rangers history. Photo courtesy of Getty Images.

Rangers brass. Having never played a game on Broadway, Brendl was shipped to the Flyers with Jan Hlavac, Kim Johnsson, and a third-round pick for Eric Lindros in August 2003.

Wayne Dillon

Selected number 12 overall in the 1974 amateur draft, Gerald Wayne Dillon posted good numbers as a center on the way up. But in the 1977–1978 season, the Toronto native sprained a knee and began an injury-filled career. He played 216 games over the next three years with the Rangers, scored 43 goals and 66 assists, and was traded to Winnipeg in 1979 for the dreaded "future considerations." He retired in 1982.

Jim Malone

Another center the Rangers liked in the first round, they took him at number 14 overall in the 1980 draft in Montreal. One hundred thirty-two players from that esteemed gathering (62.8 percent of those selected) made it to the NHL. Not the 18-year-old Malone. He was the highest pick to miss. He later suffered a knee injury and became a coach in New Brunswick.

Jayson More

A gritty defenseman who was selected 10th overall in 1987, he played just one game in New York before being traded to the Minnesota North Stars for Dave Archibald in November 1989. He returned to the Rangers for 14 games in 1996–1997. In neither stint did he score a goal.

Steven Rice

At least the Rangers received something in return when Rice, selected 20th overall in 1989, was sent packing. After being the captain of Team Canada, which won the gold medal at the World Junior Championships in 1991, the center skated in 11 regular-season and two postseason games on Broadway. At the end of that 1990–1991 season, he was dispatched to Edmonton with other players for Mark Messier. Rice couldn't fill his shoes, or any others, especially when he suffered two concussions and shoulder and hand injuries. He finished his career with the Hartford Whalers/Carolina Hurricanes.

Michael Stewart

Chosen number 13 overall in 1990, Stewart, a defenseman from Calgary who attended Michigan State University, spent three years with the Binghamton Rangers and never touched the Garden ice in a regular-season game. He did prove productive, however, as part of a deal in 1995, when he was traded to Hartford with Glen Featherstone for Pat Verbeek.

Peter Ferraro

The 24th pick in 1992, Ferraro's distinction is this: he and his twin brother Chris were the first set of identical twins to play on the same NHL team when they skated with the Rangers in 1995–1996. Peter was with the Rangers for just five games that season, two in the next, and one in 1997–1998. The 5'9" center/right wing, who was born in Port Jefferson, Long Island, later joined the Bruins, but spent much of the later days of his career on a long tour of the minors, from Syracuse to Peoria.

Christian Dube

Okay, he was selected early in the second round in 1995, not in the first. But the Rangers swung and missed there as well. Dube, who was born in Quebec, played as a youngster in Switzerland, where his father was a pro. After playing just 33 games as a Ranger between 1996 and 1999, scoring one goal and registering one assist, the right wing returned to the Alps. Bern, baby, Bern.

Jeff Brown

Not to be confused with the Jeff Brown who played 700 games with the St. Louis Blues and other clubs, this Jeff Brown, a 6'1", 232-pound Ontario native who starred in juniors with the Sudbury Wolves, was drafted 22nd by the Rangers in 1995. He never rose beyond the minors and played zero games with the Rangers. Call it coincidence or a hard lesson learned, the Rangers didn't select a defenseman in the first round for another nine years.

Jamie Lundmark

Another 1999 miscalculation. The Edmonton native was chosen ninth overall and garnered these accolades from Rangers coach John Muckler: "Jamie is going to be the complete package. He's going to be a very good player in this league for a long time." Oops. Give the man a mulligan. Lundmark never blossomed.

He played 114 games as a forward with the Rangers—virtually all of them between 2002 and 2004—and potted 10 goals and dished out 19 assists. Wow. He spent a brief time in Phoenix and was last seen playing in Russia.

The Ugly

Hugh Jessiman
In a deep 2003 draft, Jessiman was selected number 12. A 6'6" forward, Jessiman was a product of Dartmouth and Connecticut prep schools. As of the start of the 2007–2008 season, he hadn't even made a significant contribution in the American Hockey League. What haunts the Rangers is that rising stars Zach Parise (Devils), Ryan Getzlaf and Corey Perry (Ducks), and Mike Richards (Flyers) were all on the draft board when Big Hugh was chosen.

HURTIN' FOR CERTAIN: THE MAJOR INJURIES

Ulf Nilsson
To this day, Rangers fans hate Denis Potvin for his borderline illegal blow that KO'd the Swedish star Nilsson, who was in his first season with the team after leaving the World Hockey Association.

In the February 25, 1979, game at Madison Square Garden, the Islanders defenseman checked Nilsson, breaking his ankle and knocking him out for the rest of the season. The Rangers managed to eliminate the Islanders, but Nilsson was unable to help the Rangers during their run to the 1979 Stanley Cup Finals. Although Nilsson played just over half of the 1979–1980 and 1980–1981 seasons, he was only a shadow of his 1978–1979 self. It was a classic case of expectations unfulfilled.

Bill Gadsby
On Thanksgiving Eve 1954, the Rangers traded Allan Stanley and Nick Makoski for Gadsby and Pete Conacher. "Gadsby was a star, and in the first game, the Rangers were leading the Bruins something like 5–2, and with about a minute left in the third period, the puck goes to Bill Quackenbush of the Bruins at the point," recalled hockey historian Stan Fischler, who worked for the Rangers at the time. "He takes a shot, Gadsby goes down to block it and breaks his jaw. We didn't win a game in the month of December, and we were gone, out of the playoffs by the time the new year came. Devastating."

37

Mike Richter

Mike Richter was 35 when a damaging blow led to the end of the career of one of the greatest U.S.-born goalies.

On March 22, 2002, in the first period of a game against Atlanta, Richter was struck on the side of the head by defenseman Chris Tamer's rising slap shot. It fractured his skull, gave him a concussion, and he sat out the last nine games of the season.

But after recovering, Richter returned to play the following season, and on November 5, Oilers center Todd Marchant accidentally hit him in the forehead with his knee, causing another concussion. Richter retired on September 4, 2003, as the Rangers' all-time leader in wins (301) and games (666) by a goalie.

Jean Ratelle

The silky center broke his right ankle 17 games before the end of the 1971–1972 season during a March 1 game against the California Golden Seals at the Garden. "I was in front of the net to screen the goalie," said Ratelle, who had 46 goals at the time. Teammate Dale Rolfe fired the shot that hit Ratelle.

"It was a freak accident...I was out six weeks," he later recalled. "Bobby Rousseau played with Vic and Rod. I came back for the Finals, but I wasn't in good shape." The Bruins beat the Rangers in six games.

Emile Francis said: "That injury probably cost us the Stanley Cup. With Jean, we were right there, without him, [Bobby] Orr took control, and the Bruins won. It was a shame."

Ratelle had 491 career goals and missed getting to 500 in large part because of those lost weeks and because, early in his career, he was shuffled back and forth between the Rangers and the AHL Baltimore Clippers.

Brendan Shanahan

With the Rangers battling for a playoff spot with 23 games to play in the 2006–2007 season, the team's top scorer and inspirational leader Brendan Shanahan was heading toward the bench, turned to watch the play develop, and didn't see the Flyers' Mike Knuble

Mike Richter had a memorable career with the Rangers before sustaining concussions in 2002 and 2003.

curling away from his bench. The sudden collision sent Shanahan flying, and he lay motionless and unconscious on the ice for a few minutes before being wheeled off on a stretcher. Shanahan's recovery from symptoms took weeks, and the Rangers fell out of the race for the Atlantic Division title. Knuble didn't fare much better. He underwent surgery for a broken orbital bone and cheekbone and was lost for the season.

THE COSTS OF A DIFFERENT DRAFT

After the Rangers won the Stanley Cup in 1940, the winds of war tore through the globe and the NHL, leaving many changes in their wake.

"December 7, 1941," said hockey historian Stan Fischler, referring to the Japanese bombing of Pearl Harbor. "It was an event that stripped the team, a terrific team that had won the Stanley Cup in 1940. Neil and Mac Colville and Alex Shibicky were a great line. Neil Colville was the only guy who came back, and he came back as a defenseman."

Most NHLers at the time were Canadian, so the Colvilles and Alf Pike, a playmaking center, played two seasons, 1943–1944 and 1944–1945, with the Winnipeg Royal Canadian Air Force team, and returned to the Rangers for two more seasons in 1945. Kilby MacDonald and Shibicky enlisted in the military and went to basic training north of the U.S. border.

Samuel James "Sugar Jim" Henry, whose NHL career began with the Rangers in 1941–1942, played all 48 games that season, winning a league high 29 games and losing only 17. He enlisted in the Canadian armed forces (as did fellow netminder Chuck Rayner) and played military hockey in Ottawa and Calgary for three years. He returned to the Rangers for 1945–1946.

The Patrick brothers, Lynn and Muzz, were born in the Great White North, in British Columbia, but were naturalized U.S. citizens. The Patricks became army men: Muzz went to Hampton Roads, Virginia, and Lynn was assigned to Camp Custer in Michigan.

Perhaps the most unusual tale involved "Fiery Phil" Watson, a center who assisted on Bryan Hextall's winning goal in Game 6 of the Stanley Cup Finals, a 3–2 defeat of the Toronto Maple Leafs that clinched the trophy.

Unsure of whether Watson could serve in Canada and be able to avoid border regulations in the 1943–1944 season, the club arranged to loan Watson to the Montreal Canadiens and received four players in exchange. It turned out to be a bad move. The depleted Rangers finished in the cellar. Watson helped Montreal to the Stanley Cup.

THE UGLY

WANNA BET?

The gambling allegations that thrust Wayne Gretzky, his wife, Janet, and former player Rick Tocchet onto the front pages in 2005 and 2006 questioned the integrity of "The Great One," arguably the highest-profile player in NHL history.

But the Rangers have had sordid little betting scandals in their past as well.

In October 1948, then-commissioner Clarence Campbell threw the Rangers' Billy Taylor and the Bruins' Don Gallinger out of the league for life following a police investigation that uncovered that the two bet on at least one Bruins game with a Detroit racketeer.

Taylor was a 29-year-old center from Winnipeg who had won the Cup with the Leafs in 1942 and once set a record for seven assists in a game with Detroit before he was traded to the Bruins.

Gallinger, who was raised in Port Colbourne, Ontario, was offered contracts by the Phillies and Red Sox, but stuck with the Bruins, who first called him up at age 17 from his junior team. After two seasons with the Bruins, the winger joined the RCAF and graduated at the top of his gunnery class. In 1945–1946 he returned to Beantown to lead his team in scoring with 17 goals and 23 assists.

They also were guys who would bet $500 on a cut of a deck of cards, teammates said.

Enter James Tamer, whose gang had held up the Citizens Commercial and Savings Bank in Flint, Michigan, in 1934 and fled with $53,000. Tamer was arrested five years later, confessed, and was sentenced to 15 to 25 years in Michigan State Prison in Jackson.

Tamer was paroled, but he was mentioned in connection with the 1937 Thanksgiving Day barroom slaying of Harry Millman, a member of Detroit's notorious Purple Gang, and in the 1945 murder of Michigan State Senator Warren G. Hooper. He was not charged in either case, but the state and local police decided to wiretap his bar at 543 Woodward Avenue in downtown Detroit to monitor alleged bookmaking and numbers-running, of which he was reportedly the city's kingpin.

On February 18, 1948, police eavesdropped on a phone call from Chicago by a man wishing to bet $1,500 on that night's Chicago-Boston game at Chicago Stadium. Soon after that call, one was placed from the bar to a hotel in New York City, a person-to-person call, apparently to Taylor, who had been traded to the Rangers two weeks before. Taylor, according to reports, bet $500 on the game. Each bet on the Hawks to win and received 2-to-1 odds.

According to *The Boston Globe*, Gallinger said that Taylor previously placed bets for them with Tamer, but with his former teammate in New York, he himself had to make the phone call that day.

The Blackhawks led 2–1, but Grant Warwick tied it late in the first period. Warwick had been acquired from the Rangers two weeks earlier in the trade for Taylor. The Bruins would go on to win 4–2.

"I never felt anything," Gallinger told the *Globe* years later. "All I knew was what was happening, that I was losing $1,500 or $3,000. And, before that game was over, I sat on that bench, and I said, 'Gallinger, you can be as hard-nosed as any son of a bitch. You've seen a lot of hard-nosers in your life, and now maybe it's your turn to be hard-nosed.'" He said he never paid the bet.

Tamer was arrested, and the players were suspended indefinitely in March. Taylor had played just two games for the

Rangers. In October Campbell handed down the lifetime suspensions. They lasted until 1970, when Campbell, after meeting Taylor at a function and hearing several pleas from Gallinger, lifted the bans.

The Taylor-Gallinger suspensions were the harshest, but they weren't the first against a Ranger.

On January 30, 1946, two years before, Walter "Babe" Pratt, an offensive-minded defenseman who played six seasons in New York and was a member of the Cup-winning Rangers in 1940 and the champion Leafs in 1945, was caught betting on NHL games and was suspended indefinitely.

Pratt, a 6'3", 215-pounder—massive for a blueliner in that era—also had won the Hart Trophy as the league's MVP in 1944. But he had developed a reputation as a partier, a man-about-town.

He admitted to placing bets but argued that he never bet against his own team. Vowing to quit, he was reinstated to the Leafs after missing nine games.

His last NHL season was with the Bruins in 1946–1947. Despite the gambling issue, Pratt was inducted into the Hall of Fame in 1966.

MURDER, INTOXICATED

He soared across the Manhattan skyline like a comet, this kid from Cranbook, British Columbia. And then crashed to earth in a Toronto airport.

The Rangers scouts drooled over Don Murdoch's consecutive 80-goal seasons with Medicine Hat of the junior league and chose him sixth overall in the 1976 draft.

In his very first NHL game, the dark-haired 19-year-old scored twice. On October 12, he set a rookie record with five goals in a 10–4 victory over the North Stars in Minnesota.

An All-Star in his first season, Murdoch was killing goalies with his speed and shot, and earned the nickname "Murder." Although he caught his skate in the boards during a Valentine's Day game and tore tendons in his left ankle, the future looked bright. In that glorious campaign, Murdoch scored 32 goals and

Too much off-ice partying left Don "Murder" Murdoch and Rangers fans looking back at what might have been. Photo courtesy of Getty Images.

added 24 assists in 59 games. But the allure of the city—and all of its possibilities available to celebrities—pulled Murdoch in.

He partied hard. He partied often. He partied too much.

"At first, I thought it was just a drinking problem," former Rangers general manager Phil Esposito wrote in his 2003 tell-all memoir *Thunder and Lightning*. Esposito claimed that he and coach John Ferguson tried to slap him sober several times. "You could smell the booze on him every morning. He'd go out on the ice half in the bag, and even in the games. Once with the Rangers, he skated into the goalpost, and they had to get him out of there."

In August 1977 Murdoch was arrested at Pearson Airport when customs inspectors found 4.8 grams of cocaine in his sock. When he went to court in Branford, Ontario, a year later, Murdoch was given a suspended sentence and fined $400.

But NHL president John Ziegler suspended Murdoch for the entire 1978–1979 season. After Murdoch appealed, Ziegler reduced it to 40 games, but the winger never recovered his skills.

The Rangers traded Murdoch to Edmonton, but he couldn't last there. At 26, his once-promising NHL career was ending after 320 games, in which he scored 121 goals and registered 117 assists.

A journey through the minors followed, where fans shouted "Spoon" when he was on the ice. He was finished as a pro at 29.

"There's not a day goes by when I don't think how it might have turned out if I'd gone someplace other than New York—to an organization that was stricter or more disciplined," he said years later. "But I have to accept blame for how it turned out, too. What if I'd been stronger?"

BILLY THE KID

Perhaps the most disgraceful episode in modern Rangers history was the signing of Billy Tibbetts to a free-agent contract in December 2002.

The Rangers' press release noted some of his hockey accomplishments.

What was missing, however, cast a shadow on the ice—and left a stain on the pages of Rangers history.

Born in Boston in 1974, Tibbetts was a standout player for the Boston Junior Bruins in 1992–1993, scoring 60 goals and 80 assists in 73 games. After drifting through the amateur ranks, he finished the 1995–1996 season with the East Coast Hockey League's Johnstown Chiefs.

But Tibbetts missed the 1996–1997 through 1999–2000 seasons. The reason: he was in prison.

When he was 17, living with his family in Massachusetts, Tibbetts was charged with three counts of statutory rape. A 15-year-old girl, reportedly drunk, was taken behind a warehouse and assaulted.

Tibbetts pleaded guilty to one count; he was given a suspended sentence. A short time later, he was convicted of assault and battery on a police officer, disorderly conduct, and intimidating a witness.

A year and four months later, he shot someone with a BB gun, violating his parole, and spent 37 months in prison. That's where he was from 1996 to 2000.

Tibbetts, classified as a sex offender, was remorseful, claimed he had rehabilitated himself, and was signed to a minor-league deal with the Penguins, who offered him a second chance. Because he had talent, he eventually made it to the NHL, dressing for 29 games in Pittsburgh in 2001–2002.

"I'm not proud of what I did," he told the *Pittsburgh Post-Gazette*. "There hasn't been a day in the last nine years when I haven't thought about it....I did my time. And I'm not the only person in the world on parole. I just happen to be the only one...in the NHL."

He was suspended twice for kneeing and fighting, but the Flyers opened their doors to him in a trade before the 2001–2002 season. He was released after nine games.

Amazingly, the Rangers acquired him next.

He was 28.

Tibbetts, who said he was a member of Alcoholics Anonymous, played 35 games for the Hartford Wolf Pack and 11 games in New York that season.

In those 11 games, he had no goals, no assists, and 12 penalty minutes. He was released after the season.

Tibbetts continued his turbulent career in the minors, rolling up penalties as an "enforcer."

THEO

The demons eventually grounded Theo Fleury.

The 5′6″ Fleury had scored 40 goals four times and won the Stanley Cup with the Calgary Flames in 1989 before the Rangers signed him to a disastrous three-year, $21 million, free-agent deal in July 1999.

In his first season with the Rangers, he had just 13 goals by February, and after missing a breakaway, he dissed Rangers fans by giving the finger to a booing crowd at the Garden.

The next season, troubled by alcohol and substance abuse, Fleury voluntarily entered the NHL's substance abuse and behavioral health program in February and missed the final 20 games of the year.

"We've had several meetings as a group, as a team, and with the coaches and Glen," Rangers captain Mark Messier said at the time. "Everybody was aware of the situation, and Theo himself made everybody aware of what he was going through."

The troubled but feisty Fleury continued to lose his temper and invoked the ire of league officials, teammates, and the front office.

"I had a conversation with Theo this season, and he's had a conversation with Gary Bettman," said Colin Campbell, an NHL vice president. "We've spent a lot of time reviewing things that Theo has done on the ice, and frankly, those things would have been unacceptable had other players done them."

Fleury was defiant.

"Like I said last night, it's totally frustrating to be on the ice skating around on egg shells, not knowing if a marginal call is going to hurt the team, while anybody on the other team can do whatever they want to me—a cross check, a stick to the face, knee me—and it's not called," he told *The New York Times*. "Enough is enough."

"He hurts the team when he's not on the ice," general manager Glen Sather said. "And he hurts the team when he's overreacting."

After scoring 69 goals in three seasons, Fleury was released. He was later signed by the Blackhawks and relapsed again.

When asked years later whether it was drugs or booze that was the problem, Fleury responded: "It was all of them, it was every single one of them that you could put your finger on."

EAST ST. LOUIS BLUES

Another embarrassing discipline problem surfaced in the 1999–2000 season. Kevin Stevens, a former Penguin who was traded to the Rangers in 1997, struggled on the ice, never coming close to the 54-goal campaign he'd had in Pittsburgh.

Then, after a game against the St. Louis Blues on January 22, Stevens was busted in an East St. Louis motel room with a prostitute and $500 worth of crack cocaine, supposedly bought with stolen meal money from the Rangers. Stevens entered the league's rehab program as well, eventually returned to the Penguins, and retired in 2002.

AVES

For a guy whose passion is to make NHL opponents uncomfortable, bad boy Sean Avery was generally relaxed after practices.

One day, wearing below-the-knee baggy red shorts, with his right foot bare and a white sock and sneaker on the left, Avery strolled casually through the hallway between the dressing room and weight room as if he had been at the Rangers' training center in Westchester for all of the 2006–2007 season—instead of for just two months since a trade with Los Angeles.

"I'm sort of basing [the year] all on how it's ending, and it's ending pretty good, getting into the playoffs," Avery said a day after the Rangers had clinched a postseason berth with a 3–1 defeat of the Montreal Canadiens. "It's been pretty successful as far as I'm concerned."

Avery, 27, had been acquired from the Kings for Jason Ward and two prospects on February 5, 2007, and arrived with more than West Coast luggage and actress Elisha Cuthbert on his arm. Along came a reputation as a relentless yapper and forechecker, an on-ice irritant who tries to get rivals off their game—in any way possible.

Sean Avery's battles with Devils goalie Martin Brodeur are legendary.

"You definitely don't want to play against him," Rangers defenseman Paul Mara said. "What he says to other people, it can be pretty brutal," said Mara, who played against Avery when he was with the Phoenix Coyotes.

Sometimes, in fact, the 5'9" winger—a Pickering, Ontario, native—has crossed the line. He was overwhelmingly named the most-hated player, with 66.4 percent of the vote, as well as the most overrated player, in a recent players' poll conducted by *The Hockey News*.

While playing for the Kings, Avery made disparaging remarks about French Canadians and was involved in an altercation in which he was accused by forward Georges Laraque, who is black, of making a racial slur, a charge Avery denied. It isn't only opponents whose wrath he has drawn. Avery was suspended in 2007 by the Kings for disputes with coaches.

"I think I'm a little more mature," Avery told *Newsday*. But not any less brash.

Avery, who was dumped by Cuthbert and then linked to other actresses in the gossip pages, had his Hollywood digs featured on MTV's *Cribs*, and his art-and-curio-filled New York apartment was photographed for a *New York Times* fashion article.

A Rangers public relations staffer hovered nearby during interviews to assure that he didn't go off the rails. While he has curbed his tongue somewhat—if not his enthusiasm—he managed to publicly call New Jersey Devils forward Cam Janssen "a meathead" and goaltender Martin Brodeur "a whiner and a big baby" for falling down after a bump as if he was shot.

Those comments came after a February 21, 2007, run-in when tempers really flared. Avery was his usual irritating self, screening Brodeur for almost two periods, then crashed into the big goalie near the end of the second while diving for a rebound. Brodeur's mask went flying, and he gave Avery a two-handed shove. Avery's response sent Brodeur to the ice, and a pileup followed. The Devils went on to win 2–1, but the feud simmered.

Naturally, Avery was idolized by some of the Garden faithful—who compared him to former pest Esa Tikkanen—and who are as animated as Avery when he's involved in a scrum, or a score. After a goal against the Flyers, he said: "The assist can go to the fans, because I just didn't want to hear them yell, 'Shoot!' So we got that over right away."

While he was sidelined for a month with a separated shoulder early in the 2007–2008 season, he spent several periods schmoozing with fans in the upper reaches of the Garden and impishly interrupting postgame television interviews with teammates. He wore Buddy Holly–style glasses for his photo in the media guide, and an Elmer Fudd–like hunting jacket in the locker room when his teammates were headed to a charity outing in collared golf-shirts.

"I REMEMBER WHAT RON GRESCHNER SAID WHEN HE RETIRED. 'THE THING I'M GOING TO MISS MOST IS SHOWERING WITH 23 GUYS.' AND THAT'S WHAT IT'S ALL ABOUT: CAMARADERIE."
—RANGERS GOALIE MIKE RICHTER, ABOUT SIX MONTHS BEFORE ANNOUNCING HIS RETIREMENT

In his first game back on the ice, his mouth picked up where it had left off. He challenged the Devils' Zach Parise to a fight and verbally sparred with Brodeur. Asked what Brodeur said to him, he answered: "His accent's too thick. I can't understand him." Avery also called David Clarkson a "boneheaded minor leaguer."

Islanders fans came to revile Avery as well. He was accused of ramming goaltender Rick DiPietro's head into the ice during a pileup, potentially reviving concussion symptoms. And one of the Islanders' "Ice Girls," who scrape the loose snow up during TV timeouts, claimed Avery was spouting obscenities about them after an exchange with Rangers goaltender Henrik Lundqvist, who refused to leave his position to allow them access.

"He talks all the time, even in the locker room," said Lundqvist. "What you see out there is pretty much who he is."

That passion and personality—as well as some surprising hockey talent—won over many of his current teammates.

"In the first game, the first practice, you could see he has a lot of skill," said Rangers captain Jaromir Jagr after Avery scored twice in a 7–2 rout of Toronto. "I was reading that the players voted him the most overrated player in the league. I think he's the most underrated player in the league. He can play any kind of game— he can fight, he's tough on defense, he can score goals. He's such a great hockey player, and nobody knows about him."

Jagr also appreciated the locker room patter from Avery, who led the league with 261 penalty minutes in 2003–2004. "He gives it to you, but he takes it, too. I laugh at it. Maybe somebody from other teams, they get mad because he told them something they don't want to hear. Some guys are too sensitive. In our country, that's normal. We've got the same kind of humor, like he does. He could be easily a Czech."

After the trade, which was endorsed by Rangers forward Brendan Shanahan, who played with him in Detroit and hangs out with him in Manhattan, Avery scored eight goals and registered 12 assists in 28 games and was credited by numerous players and coach Tom Renney as a key figure in a playoff push. "He represents a lot of things that we are becoming this season: aggressive, a team that drives to the net," said Shanahan. "So he's been a real good addition."

Said Renney: "He's got some sizzle, and we needed that as well."

But in the summer of 2007, when Avery became a restricted free agent and sought a raise, he bristled when the team took him to arbitration. During the hearings, management labeled him a "distraction" who might not be worth a lucrative raise. He received an $800,000 raise to $1.9 million, but his future ties to the team may have started to shred.

He was KO'd by a Chris Neil check in the second game of the 2007–2008 season and missed a month with a separated shoulder. He came back briefly and injured an already damaged left wrist in a fight with Darcy Tucker of the Leafs in a game before which he was involved in a pregame scrum, his second of the month. That incident prompted fines for Avery and the Rangers. He sang with owner Jim Dolan's bar band at a benefit, had a part in a movie on the life of Rocket Richard, and sat with fans in the cheap seats while recovering. Avery later had wrist surgery, but continued to agitate, facing Brodeur in the crease to block his vision in a playoff game, a mimicking that prompted the league to create a rule prohibiting that type of antics. He suffered a ruptured spleen in a playoff game against Pittsburgh and later left Broadway for the Dallas Stars, who offered him a four-year, $15.5-million contract, one that the Rangers declined to match, ending his tumultuous time in New York.

THE BRAWLS

Since hockey began on ponds and municipal rinks, the speed, emotion, and physical element often can't be contained, and play erupts into shoves, stick-swinging, and fisticuffs. Generally, the most damage is cuts and bruises. The real problems come when the battles escalate.

Take the Bruins-Rangers game at Madison Square Garden, December 23, 1979. At the time, this postgame free-for-all that spilled into the stands was labeled the "NHL's Ugliest Brawl" and still stands as one of the more infamous mêlées in all of pro sports.

The Bruins were celebrating a 4–3 victory, and Rangers goalkeeper John Davidson skated over to berate left wing Al Secord for an earlier sucker-punch of Swedish forward Ulf Nilsson. The confrontation escalated, and Boston's Stan Jonathan was struck by an object flung from the stands. Behind the Boston bench, a fan grabbed Jonathan's stick and swung it at him.

Terry O'Reilly, a gritty, no-nonsense player who acquired the nickname "Bloody" O'Reilly for earning more than 200 minutes in penalties in five straight seasons, went ballistic.

In full uniform, O'Reilly scaled the boards—and along with Secord, Peter McNab, and Mike Milbury—began pummeling nearby spectators in the seats and aisles who tried to intervene. In one bizarre moment that illustrates just how crazed the Bruins' response was, Milbury, who had been sitting in the dressing room alone, came back out and grabbed the shoe of a fan being pinned by McNab and began hitting him in the head with it. Garden security finally intervened, but trash rained on the Bruins as they filed into the dressing room.

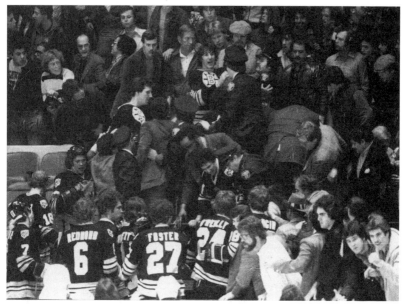

Mike Milbury of the Boston Bruins is restrained by police after charging into the stands and attempting to beat a New York Rangers fan with a shoe (which he then threw onto the ice as police approached so he would not be caught with the evidence) in New York on December 23, 1979. Photo courtesy of Getty Images.

Four people were arrested, and in the face of widespread reaction across Canada about the incident, the NHL suspended O'Reilly for eight games and Milbury for two. Critics in the government and media lamented the dangerous display and worried that the league's appeal would be forever tarnished.

Not so. The years that followed—with the coming of superstar Wayne Gretzky and the Islanders' four consecutive Stanley Cup championships—actually raised the profile of the game to new heights in the United States. And in a strange twist, O'Reilly became an assistant coach for the Rangers from 2002 to 2004.

Here are three other skirmishes that careered out of control:

1. Rangers-Islanders, 1990 Playoffs
With 1:25 left in the third period, a clean check from Rangers defenseman James Patrick on the Isles' Pat LaFontaine, who was coming into the Rangers' zone, triggered a free-for-all that epitomized the long-running rivalry. LaFontaine bounced off Patrick

and into the Rangers' Chris Nilan and ended up flat on his back with a concussion. The Islanders were livid but waited until only two seconds remained on the game clock to retaliate. Coach Al Arbour sent out enforcer Mick Vukota and Jeff Baumgartner, and everybody in the building knew what was coming. Rangers coach Roger Neilson had his players back away from the right faceoff circle where the puck was to be dropped.

Didn't matter.

When the final horn sounded, the Islanders—including goaltender Mark Fitzpatrick—bum-rushed the Rangers and attacked. Vukota administered a beat down to Jeff Bloemberg. Baumgartner and Kris King wrestled and traded punches. Nick Fotiu, in a pale yellow suit, ran down from the press box as the mêlée spilled into the benches. "This team has a great tradition, but today, the Islanders are showing no class whatsoever," said John Davidson, the former Rangers goaltender, on the MSG telecast. "What a disgrace," added partner Sam Rosen. Some Rangers fans reacted poorly, as well, rocking the ambulance taking LaFontaine to the hospital.

2. Rangers-Kings, April 4, 1981
A bench-clearing, gloves-strewn-all-over-the-ice doozy in Game 2 of the first round of the playoffs.

Among the highlights: Ranger Ed Hospodar was swinging at everything in sight, Don Maloney jumped defenseman Jerry "King Kong" Korab, and Chris Kotsopoulos took on several Kings as 267 minutes were handed out in penalties. It was the only game the Kings would win in the series.

"My God, this is serious," said announcer Jim Gordon during the havoc. "Nobody can stop it, it'll just have to wear itself out." Said Bill Chadwick, a former referee: "I've been in this league for a long, long time, and I've never seen anything worse than this. This kind of thing could set the game back 10 years."

3. Rangers-Canadiens, March 16, 1947
This one started accidentally, intensified in confusion, and ended with the commissioner stepping in to order an end to the feud years later.

Kenny Reardon, a tough, Winnipeg-born defenseman, was carrying the puck up the ice when he was hit by the Rangers' Bryan Hextall and flew in the other direction into the Rangers' Cal Gardner, whose stick blade cut Reardon's lip. As Reardon walked through the Garden passageway toward the locker room for repairs, a drunken fan apparently tried to lunge at him. Reardon swung his stick at the irritant, and Garden cops jumped on Reardon.

The Rangers bench stood up to see what the commotion was about behind them, and across the ice, the Canadiens thought the Rangers might have been messing with their teammate. The Montreal bench emptied, players paired off, and a 20-minute donnybrook ensued.

All the while, Reardon was in the trainer's room, avoiding the ruckus.

Once peace was restored, there was still ill will between Reardon and Gardner.

In a *Sport* magazine article years later, Reardon warned that Gardner should always watch his back, because he would eventually retaliate. That threat concerned NHL Commissioner Clarence Campbell enough for him to require that Reardon post a bond and never attack Gardner, and the tension dissolved.

Leaping Lou Meets Mr. Hockey

One of the NHL's greatest players—indeed, many call him "Mr. Hockey"—Gordie Howe of the Detroit Red Wings, was one of the combatants in the most memorable fight in Rangers history.

The Rangers were a feisty team in the 1958–1959 season—one that would end in a shocking collapse—and the toughest, drop-the-gloves-and-let's-go guy on Broadway was Lou Fontinato, a 6'2", 220-pound defenseman from Guelph, Ontario, who wore No. 8 and played with a snarl.

Fontinato, who debuted with the team in 1954, delighted the Garden faithful, who dubbed him "Leaping Lou"—mostly for his crunching body checks that began when he left his feet before impact, but also for his penchant to jump straight in the air while protesting his penalties to the officials. And there were plenty of infractions: Fontinato led the NHL in the 1955–1956 and 1957–1958 seasons, mostly compiled from fighting and misconduct penalties.

In turn, Fontinato loved the fans in the bustling Big Apple of the mid-to-late 1950s. "I like the ravioli, and I like the people," he said in his rookie season. "They all look like paisans."

But no opponents were paisans for Fontinato, especially Howe.

When the Rangers hosted the Red Wings at Madison Square Garden on February 1, 1959, Howe—no shrinking violet himself—smacked forward Eddie Shack in the ear with his stick. A scrum ensued, and as the refs were calming things down, Fontinato erupted.

He flew in from mid-ice and sucker-punched Howe with three lefts to the head.

Not a good idea, as it turned out. Howe landed five punches that sent Fontinato first to the ice, crumpled and bloodied, and then to the hospital.

Howe lunged and, grabbing Fontinato by the throat with his right hand, unloaded a single left that collapsed Fontinato's cheekbone. Fontinato was dazed, and while still holding him, Howe's next punch broke Fontinato's nose. A third left sliced a cut over his eye. A fourth busted open his lips. The last blow, a short right, felled Fontinato. One of the Rangers, who watched the demolition in awe, later said Howe's punches "sounded like an axe splitting wood."

The fight gained notoriety around the country when the battered and bleeding Fontinato was displayed in a huge picture in *Life* magazine. In perhaps one of the greatest public-relations spins of all-time in sports, Herb Goren, the Rangers' press agent, declared: "What they don't show was all the body blows Louie got in." Fontinato eventually recovered and would play two more seasons with the Rangers. In his six-year career in New York, he averaged more than a penalty a game—a total of 939 minutes in 418 contests.

Fontinato was traded to the Canadiens for Doug Harvey in the summer of 1961, and his punishing style led to the end of his

career. In 1963 he was forced to hang up his skates—and fists—
after suffering a neck injury while checking Vic Hadfield during a
March 9 game against his former team—the Rangers.

Fotiu Too

A decade later, the player who filled Fontinato's role was a native
New Yorker—Staten Island–born Nick Fotiu—who was the first
Ranger raised in the city. A popular and emphatic enforcer, the left
wing didn't even play organized hockey until he was 15, but he
became a deceptive skater with a decent wrist shot.

His quick hands and rambunctious attitude, however, are
what attracted him to Rangers general manager John Ferguson
in 1976, who brought him to the NHL after slogging through
teams such as the Cape Codders of the North American Hockey
League and the New England Whalers of the World Hockey
Association.

Fotiu had grown up watching Rangers games from the upper
reaches of the Garden—the least expensive "blue" seats—and he
never forgot his roots. During pregame warmups, he would fling
pucks high into those sections, and the souvenirs were treasured.

But Rangers devotees also cherished Fotiu—a former con-
tender for the state's Golden Gloves awards—for his
pugnaciousness.

Fotiu's most notable bouts were with the Flyers' Behn Wilson;
the Blues' Steve Durbano, when he chased him up through the
tunnel between the benches; and in a 1979 preseason game with
the Flyers' Jim Cunningham.

Heavyweight Champion Goes Down

Tie Domi, who was acquired from the Leafs in June 1990, also
made his mark on the roster of Rangers rumblers. With New York,
the demonstrative Domi, whose eyebrow hair stretched across his
forehead in one line, had two memorable scraps with one of the
toughest fighters of his era, Bob Probert of Detroit.

"One that sticks out, and it was a big thing, was when I fought
Domi, our second fight in New York," Probert said. "He had cut
me over the eye in the first fight and did this thing with his

Native New Yorker Nick Fotiu's willingness to do the dirty work made him a valuable, and beloved, player for the Rangers. Photo courtesy of Getty Images.

hands, like he was wearing the heavyweight championship belt. After the second fight, when I beat Domi, I looked over at our bench, and there was Steve Yzerman, standing on the bench, giving the heavyweight belt sign with his hands."

No Defense for Not Defending Defenseman

Perhaps the most shameful incident occurred in Game 7 of the second round of the 1973–1974 playoffs against the Flyers, known as the "Broad Street Bullies" at the time. Dale Rolfe was a steady, if mild-mannered, defenseman for the Rangers. Dave Schultz, known as "the Hammer," whipped Rolfe early in the decisive game, and no Ranger came to his defense. The Flyers won the series, and the incident marked the end for that particular collection of Blueshirts.

Not Just a Goon

One of my personal favorites among the other top fighters in Rangers history was Orland Kurtenbach, who wasn't just a goon. The big center from Saskatchewan could play—and punch like a heavyweight.

Kurtenbach, who played with Toronto, Boston, and Vancouver, was a Ranger for the 1966–1967, 1968–1969, and 1969–1970 seasons. He had spinal fusion and played only two games in 1968–1969.

In 639 NHL games, Kurtenbach scored 119 goals and added 213 assists. Oh, and racked up 628 penalties.

If Kurtenbach connected, one swing and the unlucky opponent was out cold. Like many veteran fighters, Kurtenbach's reputation was such that some players avoided him. During one game at the Garden, Kurtenbach plastered "Cowboy" Bill Flett of the Flyers with a check. Flett scrambled to his feet, threw down his gloves, and turned around. When he realized that the instigator was the feared Kurtenbach, Flett sheepishly collected his gloves and skated away.

The rest of my top tough guy list? Andy Bathgate, Steve Vickers, Vic Hadfield, Curt Bennett, Ron Harris, Ted Irvine, Chris Nilan, Reggie Fleming, and George McPhee.

IT AIN'T OVER 'TIL IT'S OVERTIME

Whenen Yogi Berra declared, "It ain't over 'til its over," the Yankee icon and master of the malaprop could easily have been talking about sudden-death in the NHL.

And the Rangers have been involved in some doozies.

PETE BABANDO: RANGERS KILLER

On April 23, 1950, little-used forward Pete Babando carved himself a place as a legendary Rangers-killer.

Game 7 of the Stanley Cup Finals between the Rangers and the Red Wings was a classic. The series was tied at three games apiece—and at the end of regulation, the game was tied at 3. The first overtime passed, and the second one began.

The Rangers attacked but couldn't score. The Wings came back and forced a faceoff in the Rangers' zone, where Chuck Rayner guarded the New York net.

"We were at a faceoff in their end to Rayner's right," Babando recalled in an interview with Mike Gibb of *The Hockey News* decades later. "I was playing with Gerry Couture and George Gee, who took the faceoff. Usually, George had me stand behind him. But this time, he moved me over to the right and told me he was going to pull it that way. I had to take one stride and get it on my backhand. I let the shot go, and it went in." The fateful shot, past a screened Rayner, crossed the line at the 8:30 mark.

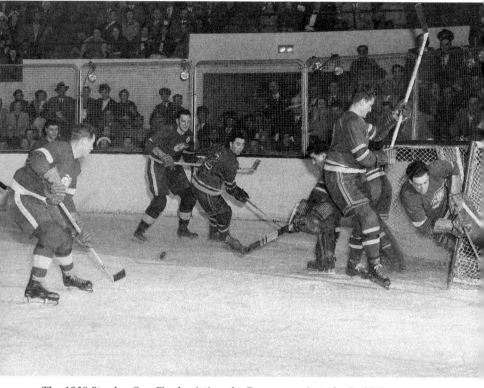

The 1950 Stanley Cup Finals pitting the Rangers against the Red Wings were among the most memorable in team history.

The Rangers would not win a Stanley Cup until 1994.

"Not a day goes by that I don't think about that goal," Rayner said long after.

In an unusual footnote, Babando was traded to the Blackhawks the following season, and in 1953 was shipped to the Rangers, where he finished his NHL career. He scored four goals in 29 games. But the one in 1950 haunted the franchise forever.

THE RISE OF THE ISLANDERS

Babando's goal was a crusher for the Rangers. And it was another extra-stanza goal against the Blueshirts in 1975 that raised the lowly Islanders' profile.

The Islanders were in the playoffs for the first time, and everyone was predicting that the Rangers would sweep the first two games of the first-round, best-of-three series.

But the teams split and were back at Madison Square Garden.

The Rangers fell behind 3–0, and goalie Gilles Villemure was replaced by Eddie Giacomin, who scrapped with the Isles' Garry Howatt and helped sparked the Rangers to tie the game.

Just 11 seconds into the extra session, J.P. Parise scored, eliminating the favored Rangers, sending the crowd into a deathly silence, and lifting the Islanders to one of the biggest upsets in Stanley Cup history.

In 14 seasons with Toronto, Boston, Minnesota, the Islanders, and Cleveland, Parise scored 27 goals in the playoffs. None was more stunning to the Rangers.

ISLANDERS STRIKE AGAIN

In the fifth game of the 1984 playoffs, an Islander struck again in OT.

This time the culprit was defenseman Kenny Morrow, a member of the gold-medal-winning U.S. Olympic team famous for the "Miracle on Ice," who inflicted the damage at 8:56 of overtime at the Nassau Coliseum.

Morrow, who looked almost wolf-like, lanky and bearded, had scored just three goals in the regular season.

A controversial goal by the Rangers' Don Maloney with 39 seconds left in regulation had tied the game. Maloney batted in a high rebound past goaltender Billy Smith. The Islanders protested, charging that Maloney's stick was above shoulder height, but the goal stood.

In the extra session, Mikko Leinonen almost won the game for the Rangers, but fanned on the puck near an open net on Smith's rebound.

Then John Tonelli dug the puck loose along the left boards in the Rangers' zone, and passed it to Morrow at the right point. Morrow's slap shot—not a blast by any means—got past screened goalie Glen Hanlon.

The Rangers were eliminated again.

THE BITTER TASTE OF LOSING IN OT

After four years of missing the playoffs, the Rangers succeeded in landing a berth in the 1966–1967 season. But they didn't last long and were eliminated on an overtime goal.

John Ferguson was one of league's top enforcers, a crease-crashing left wing who would drop the gloves regularly. He had two fights with the Bruins' Ted Green in his first game as a rookie and was the unofficial heavyweight champ of the league in that era. But he could score as well.

In the first round, with Ed Giacomin—who had nine shutouts in the regular season—in goal, the Rangers lost the first two games in Montreal and Game 3 at the Garden.

On April 13, 1967, Ferguson would wield the broom for the sweep in Game 4.

With the score tied at 1, Ferguson went around defenseman Arnie Brown and scored at 6:28 of overtime, capping another bitter loss and another long night.

HEBENTON A HERO

So often in overtimes, an unsung hero grabs the limelight.

On March 28, 1957, it was Andy Hebenton's moment.

With more than 15,000 fans roaring at Madison Square Garden, the score was tied at 2 in Game 2 in the Stanley Cup Finals against the Montreal Canadiens.

Red Sullivan came through center ice and fed the puck to Hebenton on right wing. Hebenton fended off a check from defenseman Bob Turner and bore down on Habs goaltender Jacques Plante. His backhander found a small gap between Plante's left shoulder and the crossbar. The Finals were tied at a game apiece.

Hebenton's goal secured the first overtime playoff win at the Garden in 17 years, since Alf Pike won the opener of the 1940 Finals against the Maple Leafs.

Pike's goal helped propel the Rangers to the Cup. Not so for Hebenton.

The Rangers lost the next three games.

PIKE'S PLACE

Speaking of Alf Pike, let's not forget the crafty third-line center, who skated between Dutch Hiller on the left and Clint "Snuffy" Smith on the right.

Pike was a playmaker, not a scorer, so April 3, 1940, was a significant day in his career.

At 15:30 of overtime in Game 1 of the Finals, Pike beat Turk Broda for a 2–1 win.

THE POLISH PRINCE

No discussion of overtime heroes would be complete without mentioning the short, sweet reign of "the Polish Prince," Pete Stemkowski.

In the 1970–1971 Stanley Cup semifinal, "Stemmer" scored not one, but two overtime goals against the Blackhawks, and the second was one for the record books.

He provided the winner at 1:37 of overtime in Game 1, and staved off elimination with a magic moment in Game 6, with the Rangers down three games to two.

This time, it took far, far longer.

On April 29, 1971, the teams battled through two overtimes—an extra 40 minutes—before Stemkowski scored against Hawks goalie Tony Esposito for a 3–2 game-winner at 1:29 of the third overtime.

"We were both on fumes at that point," Stemkowski recalled. "But I always had the philosophy that if my legs were heavy and I was tired, I had to feel that the guy that was wearing the other jersey had to feel just as tired as I was....We were kind of like two boxers...throwing jabs at each other. Somebody's got to fall down eventually. Chicago threw a couple of right hooks at us, where [Stan] Mikita hit the post, and I think Bill White came in and hit the crossbar. Those were two times when they could have won the game in the overtime."

Finally, Ted Irvine launched a shot at Esposito from the left faceoff circle. Stemmer was in the slot and swiped it in.

The Polish Prince, Pete Stemkowski, scored two overtime goals against the Blackhawks in the 1971 Stanley Cup playoffs. Photo courtesy of Getty Images.

"I think we were all in a fog basically at that point, and I just happened to be in the right spot and shot the puck. It went in, and I had no idea that it went in until everybody started cheering and jumping off the bench."

The goal ended a game that was the longest in Rangers history, and in its "50 Greatest Moments in Madison Square Garden History" the MSG Network ranked it number 18.

OVERTIME FIESTA

Without a doubt, the 1940 Stanley Cup Finals was an overtime fiesta.

The Rangers' Alf Pike won Game 1 against Toronto 2–1 in overtime.

Muzz Patrick's double-overtime goal in Game 5 gave the Rangers another 2–1 win.

Amazingly, neither were the most memorable of the tight series.

The next game put the exclamation point on winger Bryan Hextall's legacy.

In Game 6, Hextall, who led the NHL in goals that season, took a pass from Dutch Hiller and beat Walter "Turk" Broda at 2:07 into overtime for a 3–2 win that clinched the series 4–2 and gave the Rangers their third Stanley Cup, the first since 1933.

"I went into the corner to dig out the puck and passed it to Hextall, and he scored to give us the Cup," said Hiller. "Greatest moment of my career."

SUDDEN DEATH

In 1938 the New York Americans were the second-sister team to the Rangers.

But Lorne Carr wrote the script for their most telling victory.

Carr, who later won two Stanley Cups in Toronto, scored in the third overtime on March 27, 1938, for a 3–2 win at the Garden to capture the best-of-three series, which had been tied at one.

For his tally, he was nicknamed "Sudden Death."

That turned out to be a misnomer: when he died at age 95 in June 2007, he was believed to be the oldest living former NHL player.

SO MUCH FOR SUPERSTITION

After the conclusion of regulation play between the Rangers and Devils in Game 7 of the Eastern Conference Finals in 1994, long before Stephane Matteau scored one of the most memorable goals in NHL playoff history, the Rangers forward admitted to tapping the Prince of Wales Trophy with the blade of his stick.

No one is supposed to touch the conference trophies before the Stanley Cup winner has been decided.

Didn't affect Matteau's touch.

His wraparound from the left side of rookie goalkeeper Martin Brodeur at 4:24 of the second overtime—his second double-overtime winner of the hard-fought series—triggered an exuberant reaction from broadcaster Howie Rose, who shouted "Matteau, Matteau, Matteau!" a cry that is remembered and mimicked to this day.

Lest we forget, Matteau ended Game 3 with a score at 6:13 of the second overtime in East Rutherford, New Jersey, for a 2–1 series lead.

With the incredible Game 7 goal, the Rangers advanced to the Finals and defeated the Vancouver Canucks in another seven games for their first Cup since 1940.

GIVING THE DEVIL HIS DUE

It was the greatest series ever between the Rangers and New Jersey Devils: the 1994 Eastern Conference Finals. Three of the seven games went into double-overtime.

Coming into the series, the Rangers had edged the Washington Capitals in five games; the Devils, who were trying to advance to their first Stanley Cup Finals, had ousted the Boston Bruins in six games, winning four in a row. The Rangers were in a drought: they hadn't sniffed the Finals since 1979.

Mark Messier puts the puck past New Jersey Devils goaltender Martin Brodeur during the third period at Meadowlands Arena on May 25, 1994. Messier scored three third-period goals to give the Rangers a 4–2 win and tied the Eastern Conference Finals at three games apiece.

Game 1: In a delirious Garden, Devils forward Claude Lemieux tied the game at 3 on a scramble in front of New York goaltender Mike Richter with a minute remaining. The Devils won on Stephane Richer's breakaway goal at 15:23 of the second overtime.

Game 2: Richter's 4–0 shutout—the largest margin of victory in the series—ties things up at 1 at the Garden.

Game 3: A goal by the Rangers' Stephane Matteau at 6:13 of the second overtime proves to be the 3–2 game-winner in the Meadowlands.

Game 4: The Devils exact revenge at home and grab this one 3–1.

Game 5: Back at the Garden, the Devils go up 3–2 in the series with a 4–1 victory over the oddly listless Rangers.

Game 6: May 25. The Guarantee. "We know we have to win it, And we can win it. And we are going to win it." That's what Captain Mark Messier told the newspapers. Printed words became mythology. New Jersey led 2–1 after two periods. But, incredibly, Messier scored a natural hat trick in the third period—the last one in an empty net—to give the Rangers an incredible 4–2 win.

Game 7: Two days later, the Garden hosted a goaltending battle between New Jersey's Martin Brodeur and Richter. With the Rangers ahead 1–0, Devils forward Valeri Zelepukin knotted the score with a measly 7.7 seconds remaining in regulation. For the third time, the two sides battled into double overtime. Amazingly, it was Matteau who scored on a wraparound at 4:24 to vault the Rangers into the Finals with a 3–2 win.

"ROSIE, ROSIE!"

When Stephane Matteau scored in double overtime to beat the Devils in Game 7 in 1994, Howie Rose's call of "Matteau, Matteau, Matteau!" immediately became part of Rangers lore.

On April 29, 2007, after Michal Rozsival, playing with an injured left knee, ended an epic matinee at 16:43 of the second overtime against the Sabres with a one-timer from the right point, the chants of "Rosie, Rosie!" at Madison Square Garden sounded almost as sweet.

In the longest Rangers postseason game in 36 years—since Pete Stemkowski scored the winner in three overtimes to beat the Blackhawks on this date in 1971—the Rangers prevailed on guts and grit to win 2–1 and cut the Sabres lead in the best-of-seven Eastern Conference Semifinals in half by the same margin.

With Game 3 and essentially the series hanging in the balance, Rozsival, who was knocked out of Game 1 when checked by Ales Kotalik and didn't even practice, stepped into the spotlight. He took a pass from Michael Nylander along the wall, looked down because the puck was bouncing on the softening ice, and fired.

"I was just focusing and watching the puck the whole way," said the Czech defenseman, who didn't even see the puck go past Ryan Miller (44 saves), kiss the far post, and go in. "Everyone was jumping on me, I don't remember anything. This one was one of the lucky shots...yeah, the biggest goal of my career."

On the bench, said Brendan Shanahan, "We had a great view....It was perfect. There was traffic in front, and the one place he could put the puck, he put it there. We were getting to our feet before the puck even went into the net. He's a warrior, and we need guys like Rozsival in the playoffs."

Warrior indeed.

Rozsival blocked eight shots, played 38:16, including 10:18 shorthanded as the Rangers' penalty-killers snuffed out eight of nine power plays, including two in overtime. The goal was his third of the postseason.

"That's what champions look like," said Rangers coach Tom Renney, who knew that going down 3–0 to the Sabres would have meant an impossible gap to bridge. "My guess is he won't be the only guy aching and sore. I think we had an incredible resolve you need to win hockey games against good opponents, and the intangibles."

DRURY DAYS

Call it 7.7 seconds, Zelepukin redux.

In May 2006, leading 1–0 on a goal by Martin Straka with 3:19 left in regulation, the Rangers looked to seal Game 5 in Buffalo and send the Eastern Conference Semifinals back to MSG with a 3–2 lead.

The Buffalo Sabres had won the regular-season title, but the Rangers hoped to return to the Garden and win Game 6 for a chance to go to the Eastern Conference Finals for the first time in nine years.

Instead, the 1–0 Game 5 lead vanished when Chris Drury, standing at an angle to the right of Henrik Lundqvist, hammered in the rebound of a Thomas Vanek shot to tie the score with 7.7 seconds left as the HSBC Arena erupted. It was familiar territory for Drury, a Connecticut native and clutch performer who won a Little League World Series, an NCAA championship, and a Stanley Cup.

"The puck can find him," Buffalo coach Lindy Ruff said afterward. "He has a knack for being in the right place at the right time. He doesn't miss many of those opportunities." It was eerily reminiscent of Devil Valeri Zelepukin's goal with 7.7 left to tie the score at 1 in Game 7 of the 1994 Eastern Conference Finals.

The Rangers then lost at 4:39 of overtime when Maxim Afinogenov's 45-foot slapper on a power play went off Jed Ortmeyer's stick and through Lundqvist for the game-winner.

The stunned Rangers dropped Game 6 at MSG.

"That's the difference between champions and losers," said Jaromir Jagr. "Whatever it was, if we had it, we could have gone all the way. Maybe not all the way, but next round for sure. Compare it to baseball: we were missing the closer; we didn't have Mariano Rivera."

They did prevent Drury from duplicating the agony.

But they paid dearly.

Just two months later, Drury—an unrestricted free agent—accepted the Rangers' offer of a five-year, $35.25 million contract.

COLLAPSING UNDER PRESSURE

On March 27, 1988, a penalty shot set the stage for one of the Rangers' biggest regular-season collapses.

Devils forward Pat Verbeek duped Rangers goaltender John Vanbiesbrouck on the play, helping New Jersey, which had never made the Stanley Cup playoffs since their inception in 1982, to the last postseason berth in the Patrick Division.

The Rangers had made the playoffs for 10 straight seasons, but Verbeek, who scored a club record 46 goals that year, changed all that. A week later, on the last day of the season, the two teams were tied for that last spot—fourth place—in the six-team Patrick Division.

The Rangers hosted the Quebec Nordiques at the Garden; the Devils were in Chicago to take on the Blackhawks. If the Devils beat Chicago, they would earn the playoff spot because, although the teams would both end the season with 82 points, the Devils held the first tie-breaker—more wins.

Verbeek scored a key goal to tie the score with eight seconds left in the second period as the Rangers watched from afar on TV after beating Quebec. John McLean scored twice, the second at 2:21 of overtime. The Rangers were out; New Jersey advanced to the playoffs for the first time in franchise history.

Another remarkable collapse was aided and abetted by the Devils.

In the 2005–2006 season, the Rangers, leading the Atlantic Division much of the year, dropped the final five games to end the regular season and lose the Atlantic Division title to the Devils by one point. New Jersey ended the year with 11 straight victories.

Injuries to Jaromir Jagr (dislocated shoulder in Game 1) and Henrik Lundqvist (strained groin) proved disastrous. The Devils swept the Rangers in four straight games, knocking them out of the postseason and stretching the losing streak to nine straight games.

But the greatest regular-season collapse, "the all-time choke" according to historian/broadcaster Stan Fischler, occurred in 1958–1959.

The Rangers led the Toronto Maple Leafs by seven points with five games to go. All they had to do was beat the Leafs in Madison Square Garden. The game was tied with five minutes to play.

The Leafs' Bob Pulford just flipped the puck in on a line change, and it somehow squirted past netminder Gump Worsley.

The Rangers kept losing, and it came down to the final night of the season, March 22.

The Canadiens brought up goaltender Charlie Hodge from the Montreal Royals, and he beat the Rangers 4–2. If the Red Wings beat the Leafs in Detroit, the Rangers would sneak in.

It was excruciating. The Wings had a 3–0 lead, but the Leafs stormed back, winning 6–4 and ousting the Rangers. Instead, Toronto went to the playoffs.

SOME GREAT DATES IN PLAYOFF HISTORY

March 7, 1928—In Game 2 of the Finals, Rangers netminder Lorne Chabot suffers an eye injury, and with no replacement on the bench, 44-year-old coach Lester Patrick leaves the bench and helps the Rangers to a 2–1 overtime win over the Montreal Maroons.

April 20, 1950—In the Finals against the Red Wings, Don Raleigh scores his second consecutive overtime goal against Harry Lumley to ice Game 5. The Wings, however, win in seven.

April 1, 1962—Rod Gilbert, called up from the minors, helps the Rangers beat the Leafs 5–4 at MSG to cut Toronto's lead to 2–1. But the Rangers lose the series 4–2.

April 15, 1971—In Game 6 of the Stanley Cup Quarterfinals, winger Bob Nevin scores at 9:07 of overtime to lift the Rangers to a 2–1 win over the Maple Leafs. It was their first playoff series win in 21 years.

April 29, 1971—Ted Irvine is stopped by Hawks goalie Tony Esposito, but Pete "the Polish Prince" Stemkowski buries the rebound from the slot for a 3–2 triple overtime win in Game 6 of the semis.

April 23, 1972—Rangers sweep Blackhawks with a 6–2 win in the Eastern Conference Finals. But the Bruins bested them in the Finals.

May 8, 1979—Rangers upset Islanders, who had won a franchise best 51 games, 2–1 in the semifinals at MSG.

April 23, 1986—Bob Brooke scores 2:40 into overtime for a 6–5 victory over the Washington Capitals to even the Eastern Conference Finals at two games. The Rangers win the series 4–2, but lose to Montreal in the Finals.

May 1, 1992—In the first round of the playoffs, the Rangers take Game 7, 8–4, with Mark Messier and Adam Graves each scoring twice.

April 18, 1994—In a 6–0 defeat of the Islanders, Mike Richter becomes the first goalie to record back-to-back playoff shutouts since Davey Kerr in 1940.

June 7, 1994—One of the greatest saves in Rangers playoff history. Vancouver's Pavel Bure is hooked by Brian Leetch on a breakaway and is

It Aint't Over 'Til It's Overtime

awarded a penalty shot. Bure dekes right and left, but Richter stops him with his right pad, and Rangers win Game 4 of the Finals.

May 12, 1995—Brian Leetch backhands the puck past Nordiques goaltender Stephane Fiset at 12:42 of overtime to give the Blueshirts a 4–3 win in Game 3 of the conference quarters. The Rangers oust Quebec in six games.

April 23, 1997—The Great Gretzky scores a natural hat trick for all the Rangers' goals in a 3–2 win over Florida in Game 4 of the quarters. The Rangers wrap up the series in the next game.

May 18, 1997—Gretzky scores a hat trick, and Mark Messier notches the game-winner as the Rangers knock off the Flyers 5–4 in Game 2 of the Eastern Conference Finals. But Philadelphia prevails to win the series 4–1.

THE ZEBRAS GIVETH—AND TAKETH

It wasn't a bad call by a referee.

It was lousy positioning by a linesman that may have cost the Rangers a chance to climb back into the Stanley Cup Finals in 1986.

Montreal beat the Rangers in the first two games. In the third game, at Madison Square Garden, tied at 3–3, Claude Lemieux's goal at 9:41 of overtime was the difference.

Before Lemieux's goal, defenseman Willie Huber "had the puck hop over his stick along the boards," said Rangers coach Ted Sator.

"Then he tripped over linesman Ray Scapinello. You can say, 'Why did it happen?' But it did."

The Rangers rebounded to win Game 4 by 2–0, but lost Game 5 and the series in Montreal, 3–1.

"The third game turned the series," said Pierre Larouche.

Sometimes a referee can forget the rules. On March 14, 1962, that helped the Rangers.

The Rangers and Red Wings were tied at 2 at the Garden, and halfway through the third period, Dean Prentice broke in alone toward the Detroit goal. Goalie Hank Bassen slid his stick at the puck to break up the rush. Referee Eddie Powers accurately awarded a penalty shot.

One problem: the rules had been changed that season. Rather than any player, only the one the infraction was committed against could take the penalty shot.

Instead, Powers permitted Andy Bathgate, a better scorer than Prentice, to shoot.

Bathgate skated in from the red line, deked Bassen, who fell face-first onto the ice, and wristed the puck into the wide-open net for what turned out to be the winning goal.

Later that season, the Rangers made the playoffs for the first time in four years.

A HARDY WITHOUT LAURELS

The date: February 28, 1978.

The place: the famed Montreal Forum.

The situation: the Canadiens hadn't been beaten in 28 straight games.

The unlikely man of the hour: Hardy Astrom, making his NHL debut.

Astrom was the Rangers third goaltender (behind John Davidson and Wayne Thomas), coming over after playing with the Swedish National Team, which had won a silver medal in the World Cup in 1977.

Incredible, but true: the Rangers won 6–3, breaking the Canadiens' streak.

"Montreal had only lost, like, six games or something," recalled Rangers defenseman Dave Maloney. "Fergie [coach John Ferguson] bought a blow-up Stanley Cup, and we carried it on the bus and on the plane home."

But like a singer who never follows up after one smash hit, Astrom's NHL career fizzled after that performance. He played three more games with the Rangers, going 1–2 and finishing with a 3.50 goals-against average, and was traded in July 1979 to the Colorado Rockies for Bill Lochead.

Out west, things weren't all peaches and cream either, as former Rockies coach and current television announcer Don Cherry once said, "First practice in Colorado, we were working on breakout drills. I shoot the puck at Hardy from the far blue line, and it goes right through his legs. 'Fluke,' I figure, so I shoot another one. Right through his legs again. 'Next drill,' I said....Actually, Hardy was a nice guy, he just had a weakness with pucks."

THE SIGHTS AND SOUNDS OF THE RANGERS

THE GARDENS

There have been four Madison Square Gardens, with a $600 million refurbishing of the arena slated to begin in 2009. The Rangers have played in two, neither of which—oddly enough—is near Manhattan's Madison Square.

The first two Gardens were ornate buildings on the site of the passenger depot of the New York and Harlem Railroad on the northeast corner of Madison Square, a park on Madison Avenue and 26th Street. In 1871 P.T. Barnum converted the first structure into "Barnum's Monster Classical and Geological Hippodrome," and it was later renamed Madison Square Garden by William Henry Vanderbilt and used for bicycle racing.

In 1890 architect Stanford White designed the second Garden, a 32-story edifice that echoed a Moorish palace with a minaret tower, an 18-foot copper statue of the goddess Diana, and a main hall—the largest in the world at the time—with permanent seating for 8,000 people and room for thousands more. It was demolished after the 1924 Democratic Convention to make way for the New York Life Insurance Building.

The third Garden, where the Rangers were born, was built in 249 days in 1925 for $4.75 million at 50th Street between Eighth and Ninth Avenues—on a depot for the city's trolleys—by boxing promoter Tex Rickard to house his matches. Its most distinct feature was the marquee above the main entrance, with abbreviations

The third Madison Square Garden, on Eighth Avenue between 49th and 50th Streets in New York City, was the Rangers' first home.

announcing the events ("Rgrs, Tomw., V/S, Tonite"). Even the name atop was shortened: "Madison Sq. Garden." And in another turn of phrase, the new hockey team was named for Rickard: "Tex's Rangers."

With 17,000 seats, Rickard's Garden was a smoky place, bristling with electricity, a block from Times Square. It evolved into a mecca in the city, presenting everything from college basketball doubleheaders to heavyweight fights to the Rangers, who played their first game on Garden ice on February 13, 1926.

The Rangers' games would start at 8:45, late enough for people to have dinner first, recalled Stan Lomax, a radio announcer of that era. "People would attend games dressed in tuxedos, and have no idea how the game was played or why players were fighting on the ice," said Lomax.

The New York Americans—the original NHL team at the Garden—and the Rangers were co-tenants for 15 years, until the Amerks disbanded before World War II.

But the Rangers' biggest in-house rival at the Garden was the Ringling Brothers and Barnum & Bailey Circus, which was crucial to the Garden's success, with two or three performances daily in the spring. In fact, when the Rangers played in the 1928 Stanley Cup Finals, the team was forced to play all games on the road (four in Detroit, and two "home games" at Maple Leaf Gardens in Toronto).

The Rangers won the series in six games despite the home-ice disadvantage.

Through the decades, the Rangers' playoff games also arrived with the aroma of the big top downstairs: elephants, hay, and musk. The team often played the role of the clowns, never securing the Stanley Cup in that building.

"We had good teams, but the things that bothered me the most were things like the rodeo, the Westminster Kennel Club, and the circus," defenseman Harry Howell said in an interview for the series *Legends of Hockey.* "The first two weeks of the season, the rodeo was booked at the Garden. The Kennel Club had dogs come in February when we were making a run at the playoffs, [meaning] two more weeks on the road. Teams like Montreal and Toronto didn't have to do things like that because hockey was number one, but hockey wasn't number one in New York at the time. It still isn't, but at least they get to play all the playoff games on home ice."

> "I WAS THE MYSTERY GUEST ON 'WHAT'S MY LINE?,' AND THE PANEL DIDN'T RECOGNIZE ME WITH THEIR MASKS ON OR OFF."
> —ROD GILBERT

Practices were also like circuses, players recalled, in a rink designed for figure skating.

"For my first 10 years, we practiced at 'Iceland,' which was on the fourth floor of the old Garden on Eighth Avenue and 49th Street. It was 160 feet long and maybe 70 feet wide with aluminum boards and mirrors all around it," Howell recalled. Andy Bathgate remembered chain-link fencing in one section. "Before my time, players would shoot the puck and break the mirrors,"

Howell said. "That's where we had to practice. You wouldn't believe what went on."

On February 11, 1968, Jean Ratelle beat Roger Crozier for the final goal in the last game at Madison Square Garden III, as it came to be known, in a 3–3 tie with the Detroit Red Wings.

Earlier that day, Bill Cook, the club's first captain and a veteran of the 1926 and 1928 Cup victories, was given the honor of scoring one final ceremonial goal, skating toward the Ninth Avenue end of the rink and sliding in the puck to rousing applause as "Auld Lang Syne" was pumped out by organist Gladys Gooding.

A week later, Ratelle won the first faceoff against Forbes Kennedy of the Philadelphia Flyers in the next Garden, the circular arena that rose above Pennsylvania Station on Seventh Avenue between 31st and 33rd Streets. Phil Goyette, assisted by Bob Nevin, scored the first goal in the new rink.

This building had its quirks, as well. Madison Square Garden III was built without a box office, and one had to be fashioned in the lobby afterward. The current Garden had a box office, but no press box, and the media were spread throughout the building in sections and suites once designed for fans. And in an engineering error, the rink was actually several floors above street level.

Cablevision, the Long Island–based corporation that owns the arena, the Rangers, and the Knicks, as well as the cable network that televises the games, is planning extensive renovations: a soaring new entrance on Eighth Avenue, more luxury suites, wider concourses, a museum, and a hall of fame. The renovations are due to be completed in 2011.

THE VOICES AND PICTURES

"He shoots, he scores!"

For decades, radio and television commentators echoed that signature line of the godfather of NHL broadcasters, Foster Hewitt, whose pioneering radio play-by-play of the Toronto Maple Leafs games beginning in the mid-1920s set the bar for all who followed.

The Canadian-born, former *Toronto Star* sportswriter is acknowledged as the dean of hockey broadcasters, followed closely by Montreal's Danny Gallivan, whom Marv Albert cites as his major influence.

Albert, a native Long Islander, of course, is perhaps the seminal radio voice of the modern era of the Rangers, beginning in the 1960s, when every game was carried on a station with a strong signal.

That wasn't always the case.

In truth, the first hockey game broadcast on the radio in New York wasn't even a Rangers game. It was the opening night game of the New York Americans, the team that preceded the Rangers as a tenant at Madison Square Garden by a year.

Garden owner Tex Rickard purchased a radio station, WWGL-AM/1420, and renamed it WMSG, to broadcast all the events at the Garden. As a general rule, hockey fans had either to stumble upon the broadcasts or learn of them by word of mouth, since the station's frequency on the AM dial (FM hadn't been invented) changed often, and newspapers treated the "new" medium with great disdain.

The coverage on February 13, 1926, wasn't of the entire game, however. Fans would not be able to tune in to complete games until 13 years later.

In those early years, the games were picked up in progress, and for 30 minutes to an hour, listeners would hear some play-by-play and a summary. Each year, the format and the number of games varied. There was no consistency on that level.

The voice of WMSG was Jack Filman, a native of Hamilton, Ontario, who was known for his rapid-fire, staccato play-by-play delivery.

"Filman made 'the world's fastest game' seem even faster," recalled Bill Cook, the Rangers' first team captain. Although how Cook would know that remains a puzzle, since he [Cook] was on the ice when Filman was working, and tape recorders hadn't been invented.

Every February 25 marks the anniversary of hockey's first televised game. The year was 1940, the Rangers versus the Montreal Canadiens at the "old" (or third) Madison Square Garden.

Sports on television is so pervasive and lucrative nowadays that it is hard to believe there was a time when "visual radio" was ridiculed and given little chance of making any significant impact.

We marvel today at the MSG Network, NBC, and others bring NHL games into our homes, complete with multiple cameras, replays, and countless innovations.

The first game ever televised was shot with one camera in a fixed position. The game probably attracted no more than a few hundred viewers. There were only about 300 television receivers in the New York area. Television manufacturers donated most of the sets to newspaper editors, critics, and advertising executives.

Some sets were purchased (the price was a hefty $660 apiece) by tavern owners. Viewers had to huddle directly in front of the set because the screen only measured seven inches across, and certainly couldn't be viewed from any distance.

The Rangers defeated Montreal that night by a score of 6–2. It was actually the third televised sporting event to appear on TV. Nine months earlier, the great Bill Stern called a college baseball game between Princeton and Columbia at New York's Baker Field. The night before the Rangers game, on February 24, the National AAU Track and Field championships were aired from the Garden.

All of the events were carried on W2XBS, the experimental station of the National Broadcasting Company, then the leader in commercial radio.

The play-by-play announcer for the first hockey telecast was Skip Walz, a noted amateur athlete of the 1930s who had also done public address work for Manhattan College football and Brooklyn Dodgers baseball. For the sports telecasts, he called himself "Bill Allen," because, he noted years later, "it seemed to roll off the tongue better."

There was little or no attention given by the press to the presence of television at the historic game. Newspapers (there were 11 of them in New York City at the time) viewed TV (and radio, as well) as a rival that could threaten circulation. Some publishers insisted that W2XBS purchase ads if it wanted to see its schedule in print. Television listings as we know them were still decades away.

At the time of the first televised game, the Rangers and the Boston Bruins were locked in a heated battle for first place in the seven-team NHL. The Bruins eventually finished first by three points.

Television, however, agreed with the Rangers. They went on to win the 1940 Stanley Cup.

Through the years, the Rangers have boasted a cornucopia of some of the greatest announcers in New York history: Marty Glickman, Bert Lee, Ward Wilson, Bud Palmer, Win Elliot, Spencer Ross, Sal Marchiano, Bill Mazer, Jim Gordon, Bill Chadwick, Mike Emrick, Tim Ryan, Howie Rose, Sal "Red Light" Messina (a former goaltender), Marv Albert, Kenny Albert, Sam "It's a power play goal" Rosen, and John Davidson, among others.

And for a single season, 1959–1960, Winnipeg-born Monty Hall, of *Let's Make a Deal* television fame, was a Rangers radio analyst.

Gordon, the play-by-play man, and Chadwick, "the Big Whistle," the NHL's first American-born referee who had lost the sight in his right eye, were a popular—if quirky—pair.

Many fans can recall Gordonesque phrases: "Three on two, if they hurry," "Save, somehow!" Or Chadwick's: "Shoot the puck, Barry," when Rangers defenseman Beck would hesitate, or this hurried call, "Great save, off his left-hand foot."

From 1967 through 1981, Chadwick—who grew up on 122nd Street and Second Avenue in Manhattan—spent four years on radio with Marv Albert, and 11 with Gordon on Channel 9.

He had begun officiating in 1939, four years after an injury in the minors. He worked until 1955, and to avoid keeping his hands in his pockets while officiating, he created hand signals when calling a penalty. Those same signs remain in use. When he retired at age 39, he said, "If you wait 'til they ask you to leave, it's too late."

In some ways, Chadwick was hockey's version of Phil Rizzuto. He once remarked on the air that Rangers center Gene Carr "couldn't put the puck in the ocean if he was standing on the beach." After Carr was traded to the California Golden Seals, he scored against the Rangers during an away game. "I thought you said Carr couldn't put the puck in the ocean," said Gordon. "Well, Jim," said Chadwick, "it's a bigger ocean out here."

Rising above all the millions of words describing the Rangers' fancies and foibles stands The Call, by Marv Albert in the summer of 1994:

"Bure and MacTavish with one and six-tenths seconds to go....The puck is dropped. MacTavish controls, and it's all over....The New York Rangers have won the Stanley Cup...something that most people thought they would never hear...in their lifetime. And the Rangers pour onto the ice to pound each other...Mike Richter being congratulated....And they are going wild at Madison Square Garden!"

THE SCENE

Before every Rangers game at Madison Square Garden, the names and seat locations of celebrities in attendance are distributed to the media gathered in the arena's press room.

After all, beginning with the team's debut at the original Garden in 1926, luminaries from the worlds of movies, television, politics, music, and sports have been frequent attendees at Rangers games.

In the early years, couples dressed in tuxes and evening gowns for dinner or a night on the town filled the most expensive seats. Today the dress is more casual, but the well-known names and faces still can be found in the often-buzzing stands, including a regular contingent of supermodels.

New York Yankees greats Lou Gehrig and Babe Ruth often showed up and were friendly with some players of that era, who often lived in hotels near Manhattan's theater district.

Gehrig, the pinstripers' "Iron Horse," even presented Murray Murdoch with a ring in an on-ice ceremony before the Rangers left wing played his 400th consecutive game. Murdoch would go on to set an NHL record of appearing in 563 straight games.

Actors Humphrey Bogart and George Raft—whose favorite player was defenseman Taffy Abel—often came to the games. TV and real-life couple Lucille Ball and Desi Arnaz were there. Cab

None other than Lou Gehrig and Babe Ruth attended many Rangers home games. In fact, Gehrig presented Murray Murdoch with a ring in an on-ice ceremony before the Rangers left wing played his 400th consecutive game.

Calloway, the jazz singer, and even the Duke and Duchess of Windsor showed up for the scene.

And just as former New York Mayor Rudy Giuliani was often in a prime box seat at Yankees games in the 1990s, Mayor Michael

Bloomberg attends games as Jimmy Walker did when he ran the city in the late 1920s and early '30s.

Christopher Reeve, the actor who played Superman, and his wife, Dana, were there. On January 12, 2006, she sang Carole King's "Now and Forever" at Madison Square Garden during the retirement ceremony for Mark Messier's Rangers jersey.

In recent years, actors Tim Robbins and Susan Sarandon have been regulars, and the list goes on: former tennis great John McEnroe and NFL quarterback Boomer Esiason have followed the team for years, as did the ukulele-playing Tiny Tim. Actor Liam Neeson and his wife Natasha Richardson, radio personality Howard Stern, actors Billy Bob Thornton, Martin Short, and Steve Schirripa of *The Sopranos* all have been on hand.

THE CHANT

At 28 years and counting, it is perhaps the longest-active two-word taunt of a player in professional sports.

No matter which team is playing the Rangers at Madison Square Garden, the whistles start somewhere in the stands. The tune sometimes sounds like the "Let's Go Band" melody, which was once played at the Garden, to signal the chant: "Pot-vin Sucks!"

The target of the chant, former Islanders defenseman Denis Potvin, is long retired, but his infamy lives on at Seventh Avenue and 33rd Street.

On February 23, 1979, Potvin zeroed in on the Rangers' Ulf Nilsson and connected with a hip check that decked the popular Swedish center. Nilsson's ankle cracked, knocking him out for the rest of the season.

Potvin wasn't penalized for the legal hit—unless you count the humiliation of being loudly slammed by a contingent of fans as continuing punishment.

At a reunion at Nassau Coliseum in 2006 for members of the Islanders teams who hoisted the Stanley Cup for the first four years of the 1980s, Potvin joked about the long-running public insult. "What are they saying? Potvin's Cups?"

WHEN THE GARDEN CHEERED FOR THE OTHER GOALIE

The boos, the obscenities, the thrown objects.

It's never pleasant to be an opposing skater at Madison Square Garden.

Except for one man on one night in 1975.

Eddie Giacomin was the Rangers' number-one goaltender for eight seasons, shared the Vezina Trophy in 1971, and led the Rangers to the Stanley Cup Finals in 1972.

Three years later, the 36-year-old Giacomin—one of the team's most popular players—was waived on Halloween night and claimed by the Red Wings.

Giacomin was told of the move by general manager Emile Francis at the team's practice rink in Long Beach, Long Island, and was shattered.

"It was like I had fallen through a trap door and was tumbling in space," Giacomin told *The New York Times*. "I walked toward the car, but didn't know whether I should stop or just keep walking, keep walking out into the water."

Three nights later, on November 2, Detroit was at the Garden, and Giacomin was between the pipes in an unfamiliar red, not blue, uniform.

As one, Rangers fans stood and chanted, "Ed-die, Ed-die!" drowning out the end of the national anthem in thunderous appreciation for his tenure. Giacomin wept behind his mask.

The fans at the Garden applauded every Giacomin save en route to a 6–4 Detroit win.

RON GRESCHNER: MORE THAN CAROL ALT'S GUY-PAL

Gresch was a pioneer.

Long before hockey players even thought of dating soap opera actresses or pop singers, as can happen today, Gresch and super-model Carol Alt were an item.

Alt and her fellow (or perhaps, more appropriately, lady) models provided eye candy at Madison Square Garden in the early 1980s. Gresch and Alt were married in 1983.

Ron Greschner raises his stick in celebration of a goal during a game against the New York Islanders in March 1984. Photo courtesy of Getty Images.

Alt, who grew up on Long Island, was on the cover of the 1982 *Sports Illustrated* swimsuit issue, and the husband-wife duo made a workout video together in 1987.

Greschner, who wore the No. 4 jersey, was a Ranger his entire career, from draft day in 1974 to his retirement after the 1989–1990 season.

An offensive-minded defenseman, Greschner scored more than 20 goals four times and is the second-highest scoring defenseman in team history. With 179 goals and 431 assists for 610 points, Greschner fills the seventh slot on the team's all-time scoring list. At the top of his game in 1977–1978, he complied 24 goals and 48 assists—72 points in 78 games, numbers that a forward would covet.

Greschner was on the 1978–1979 team that liked the night life, thundered into the Stanley Cup Finals against the Montreal Canadiens, and were leading 2–0 in Game 2 before the Canadiens turned on the heat, winning that contest and the next three.

One little-known item about Greschner. Put it under "ugly"— or at least unsanitary:

He was suspended for the final three regular-season games in 1988–1989 for the rare "abuse of an official."

On March 25, 1989, in Pittsburgh, defenseman Rod Buskas pulled Greschner's hair during a fight in the second period. Furious that the ref or linesmen had not seen the yanking, which he felt deserved a separate penalty, Greschner spit water at linesman Ron Asselstine. He was tossed from the game and barred two days later.

FROM IRELAND TO SIBERIA: THE PUBS

Before—and after—a game at Madison Square Garden, many have enjoyed a little libation. For fans, a little sip to grease the wheels, to loosen the throat before settling in for the contest; a cocktail or a frosty brew to celebrate a win or to ease the pain of a loss afterward.

In the late 1970s and early 1980s, when half the team lived in Westchester and half in Manhattan, Oren & Aretsky's uptown,

Charley O's on 33rd Street, and Herlihy's on the West Side were the preferred spots for the players' postgame revelry.

Nowadays, there is Local, an upscale pub with flat-screen TVs and a roof deck, and the Irish pub Tir Na Nog, both within a slap shot of the Garden on West 33rd Street and Eighth Avenue. You can usually find some players and media folks gathering there afterward.

A little ways south on Seventh Avenue are Mustang Harry's and Mustang Sally's, traditional sports bars, and the old Blarney Rock at 137 West 33rd always has fans wearing Rangers jerseys. So does the Molly Wee Pub at 402 Eighth Avenue. Kinsale Tavern on the Upper East Side had a good hockey crowd, as did the Blue Room up on Second Avenue. One of the best spots for steak before the game is the historic Keen's on West 36th, with its collection of clay pipes covering parts of the ceiling.

Over in Astoria, Queens, there is Bohemian Hall, with its outdoor beer garden and selection of Czech beer, where fans gathered to watch Rangers playoff games in recent years.

Then there was Siberia.

Siberia was a hole-in-the-wall, bare-bones dive with exposed wires in an unusual location: on the downtown side of the 50th Street subway station.

Siberia opened on Halloween night in 1996. Winona Ryder tended bar there once, but Tracy Westmoreland was the owner and nightly presence amid the graffiti. The windows were taped with garbage bags to keep the light out. You could feel the rumble of the trains. You'd always find Rangers fans there after games drinking vodka before heading home.

When Westmoreland was evicted in 2002, he reopened Siberia in a grungy joint at 356 West 40th Street, a rundown block with parking garages near the Port Authority. But it wasn't the same, more of a yuppie dive, with $6 beers, crummy bands, reeling drunks, and reporters from Associated Press, CNN, and the *Post*.

I went there once after a game. I remember there was no sign. The left of four unmarked doors had a red light bulb. One brick room, 25¢ stale nut and candy gumball machines, a "Playboy" pinball machine, and the best part, a classic, eclectic jukebox. Not a Rangers fan in sight. It closed in 2006.

FROM A SAVE TO A HIT

John Davidson unexpectedly spawned a rock-and-roll chart-topper in 1978.

In a playoff game at Madison Square Garden on April 13, a Buffalo player clanged a shot off Davidson's mask, and he shook his head, trying to clear his sight and shake off the cobwebs.

"I got my bell rung pretty good," Davidson recalled.

Lou Gramm and members of the band Foreigner—Sabres fans—were watching the game on television, and when they heard announcers Jim Gordon and Bill Chadwick repeatedly mention the phrase "double vision," they sat down and wrote some lyrics.

"Double Vision" was a hit, and the album sold 6 million copies.

The Rangers never struck gold. They won the game 4–3 but lost the next one—and the series.

ALMOST FAMOUS

Clark Gable, Myrna Loy…and Phil Watson?

The two movie stars were filming *The Great Canadian*, a hockey movie that Metro-Goldwyn-Mayer was underwriting. For shots at the Garden, Watson was chosen as Gable's skating double and grew a pencil-thin moustache to make it as realistic as possible. The project was eventually canceled, leaving Fiery Phil among the ashes of Hollywood's almost-famous.

RANGERS FIRSTS
AND OTHER ACHIEVEMENTS

T he eight decades of Rangers history are replete with firsts and
achievements—dubious and otherwise. Here are some of
them:

• William Osser (Bill) Cook was the Rangers' first captain and
scored the Blueshirts' first goal at 10:37 of the second period in a
1–0 opening night victory over the Montreal Maroons on
November 16, 1926.

• Two Rangers claim to be the first to employ the slap shot,
years before Boom Boom Geoffrion and Bobby Hull. Bill Cook's
younger brother Fred, known as "Bun," used the shot to surprise
goaltenders used to wrist shots in practice. Alex Shibicky, Cook's
successor at left wing on the Rangers' top line in 1936, contended
that he debuted the shot in a game. The two played together for
just the 1935–1936 season, Cook's last as a Ranger and Shibicky's
first. "Bun never used the slapper in a game," Shibicky said. "I did,
but it was his idea."

• Center Davey Kerr was the first NHL player to make the
cover of *Time* magazine on March 14, 1938. Kerr, a McGill
University grad—such an education was rare for a player at the
time—won the Vezina Trophy with a 1.54 goals-against average
and eight shutouts.

• Frank Boucher, who coached the team to its third Cup in
1939–1940, is believed to be the first bench boss to pull the goaltender on the fly in the waning minutes of a game—when the

The Rangers' first captain, Bill Cook, poses for a photo in January 1934.

Rangers were down a goal—in order to get an extra attacker on the ice, which is a common practice in the modern game.

• Boucher's innovations didn't stop there. Most teams carried one goaltender and an emergency backup. In 1945–1946 Boucher kept both Sugar Jim Henry and Chuck Rayner and created the first two-goalie rotation. Not until the 1960s did it become more common practice. Henry and Rayner would not only play in alternate games, as is the case today, but in alternate periods. And sometimes, Boucher would even change them from shift to shift as he changed his two defensemen. "We weren't crazy about that system," Rayner once recalled. "But we were roommates and best friends, so we lived with it."

• Samuel James Henry was born in Winnipeg on October 23, 1920. The nickname, Sugar Jim, came from his fondness for brown sugar, particularly on cereal. Henry played 406 NHL games and finished his career with a 2.87 goals-against average. Traded to Boston before the 1950–1951 season, Henry is also remembered in one of the most dramatic hockey photos of all time. The image showed Henry, right eye blackened, shaking hands with Maurice "Rocket" Richard, himself blood-streaked and black-eyed, following a pivotal Stanley Cup playoff game on April 8, 1952. Richard had scored an overtime goal to give Montreal a semifinal-round victory in seven games over Boston.

• Before certain rules changed, Rayner was the first goalie in history credited with scoring a goal. Playing for a Royal Canadian Armed Forces team in Halifax, Nova Scotia, in 1944, Rayner skated the length of the ice and hit the twine. Like all the goalies of his time, he played his entire career without a face mask. "I never really felt I needed a mask," he said. "Gump [Worsley, a successor as Rangers goalie] said it best: 'My face is my mask.'" The Flyers Ron Hextall would be the first NHL netminder to score, decades later, on December 8, 1987, in a 5–2 victory over the Boston Bruins at Philadelphia. Two years later, he did it again in a Flyers playoff game against Washington.

• The Rangers were the first franchise to welcome players from overseas: Ulf Sterner was the first Swede in the league in 1964–1965, opening the gates for the top two Swedish scoring sensations, Anders Hedberg and Ulf Nilsson, to come to New York in 1978; Pentti Lund was the first Finn to win an NHL trophy, the Calder Cup, for top rookie in 1948–1949. Lund did skate in two playoff games for the Bruins in the previous season.

• Vic Hadfield was the first Ranger to score 50 goals in a season. On April 3, 1972, Hadfield—posted just outside the Montreal crease—nudged in the puck past Denis DeJordy, and the Garden exploded in a three-minute standing ovation. "Believe me, I had never heard anything like that in my life," said Hadfield.

Frank Boucher led the Rangers to one of their four Stanley Cups in the 1939–1940 season.

• On December 1, 1941, four sets of brothers played in the same game. The Rangers Mac and Neil Colville and Lynn and Muzz Patrick went up against Max and Doug Bentley and Bob and Bill Carse. The Blackhawks defeated the Blueshirts 4–1 at Chicago Stadium. Dave and Don Maloney and Peter and Chris Ferraro were the Rangers' other brother acts.

• Goaltender John Vanbiesbrouck, who played for the Rangers from 1983 to 1993, is the only player in NHL history to have all five vowels in his name. "The Beezer," as he was known, was traded to Vancouver for future considerations, which turned out to be defenseman Doug Lidster (four vowels).

• The Rangers have had a Beveridge (Bill), a Schaefer (Joe) and three Millers (Kelly, Kevin, Warren), a Ching (Johnson) and a Bing (Juckes). They've had two Shacks (Eddie and Joe), a Wood (Robert), and a Park (Brad), two Carrs (Lorne and Gene), a Roman (Lyashenko), a Yip (Foster), and a Kannegiesser (Sheldon).

• Andy Bathgate scored at least one goal in 10 consecutive games from December 15, 1962, to January 5, 1963—still a team record.

• Beginning in 1952 and for 17 seasons—and 1,160 games— defenseman Harry Howell was always around. No one played more games for the Blueshirts. He played in seven All-Star Games and was awarded the Norris Trophy as the NHL's top defenseman in 1966–1967. On January 25, 1967, Howell became the first Ranger to have a night in his honor at the Garden.

ACHIEVEMENTS (SOME DUBIOUS)

• Longest losing streak: 11 games from October 30 to November 28, 1943.
• Most times shut out: 10 in 1928–1929.
• Fewest wins: 6 in 50 games in 1943–1944.
• Fewest goals: 150 in 70 games in 1954–1955.
• Most lopsided win: 12–1 at MSG on November 21, 1971, over the California Golden Seals.
• Worst losses: 15–0 at Detroit January 23, 1944, and 13–3 at home on January 12, 1944, versus the Bruins.
• Fastest three goals by an opponent: 21 seconds—the Blackhawks' Bill Mosienko in a 7–6 Chicago win in the third period on February 23, 1952.
• Fastest five goals: Bruins in 2:55 in an 11–3 rout on December 19, 1974, at Boston.
• Most saves: Mike Richter made 59 in a 3–3 tie with Vancouver on January 31, 1991.

• Four men in Rangers history were player, captain, and coach: George "Red" Sullivan, Bill Cook, Neil Colville, and Phil Esposito.

• Jean Ratelle scored the final goal at the third Madison Square Garden on February 11, 1968, a 3–3 tie with the Detroit Red Wings. A week later, on February 18, he took—and won—the first face-off in the new Garden against Forbes Kennedy of the Philadelphia Flyers. He was the first Ranger ever to reach 100 points in a season, scoring 109 in 1971–1972. In 862 career matches with the Blueshirts, Ratelle tallied 336 goals and 481 assists for 817 points. He added 42 points (nine goals, 33 assists) in 65 postseason games with New York.

• In the first Stanley Cup Finals at the fourth Garden, the Rangers beat the Bruins 5–2 on May 4, 1972.

BREAKING THE ICE

In 2006–2007 there were only a handful of blacks playing in the NHL. The Rangers had two black players on the team on opening night: veteran goaltender Kevin Weekes and rookie forward Nigel Dawes.

Weekes, a class act whose roots were in Barbados and Toronto, was a student of goaltending history, and players loved his enthusiasm on the bench. Jaromir Jagr jokingly called him "Ray," for Ray Charles. Dawes, a forward from Winnipeg, played eight games that season, but was called up again in 2007–2008 and appears to have a future in the NHL.

More than a half-century ago, the Rangers were the first team to sign a black player: Art Dorrington, from Truro, Nova Scotia, who inked a deal with the organization in 1950.

On his first trip to the U.S., the 20-year-old Dorrington was with a Connecticut minor-league team that practiced at the Garden, and a scout offered him a contract to play for the Rangers' affiliate, the Rovers, who were on a road trip.

"I was in a hotel in New York City by myself for four days, and I felt homesick," he said years later. "I got impatient, so I told the Rangers that I needed to play some hockey. They arranged for me to go to Atlantic City for a weekend tryout with a team that they had a working agreement with."

No black had played pro hockey in the U.S. until the 5'8" Dorrington spent eight years with Atlantic City Sea Gulls of the Eastern Hockey League, scoring 151 goals and 152 assists for 303 points in 336 regular season games. In 1951 the Gulls won the league championship, and Dorrington had 18 goals and 16 assists. In the summer, he played center field for teams in the Boston Braves organization in upstate New York.

Dorrington played for six different Eastern League teams. He scored 25 goals for the Johnstown Jets in 1952–1953 and 30 goals in 1953–1954. With the Washington Lions, he had 33 goals and 35 assists in 1954–1955, and 30 goals and 31 assists for the Philadelphia Ramblers in 1955–1956.

"I went to places in the Eastern League like Washington, D.C., Baltimore, Charlotte, Greensboro, and the rest of the team would go into a hotel or a restaurant, and I wouldn't be allowed to go in. I had to put up with the same kind of racism that Jackie Robinson put up with in baseball," he told reporters after he had settled back in Atlantic City when his career was over to run a youth hockey foundation.

Dorrington, who had become a U.S. citizen, was drafted in 1956 and rejoined the Ramblers in 1958, where he played just 11 games. During a game in Utica, he was tripped while carrying the puck and broke his left leg.

After four operations, he quit in 1961. "I lost my speed," he once recalled. "I didn't consider [the injury] a racial thing. I don't. I just beat a guy on a play, and he stuck his leg out. Most of the Eastern League players were Canadians. We had more in common than not."

THE CENTURY CLUB

Only six players have scored 100 or more points in a season:

Jaromir Jagr, 123

Jagr had some monumental seasons in Pittsburgh, playing with Mario Lemieux. But in the 2005–2006 season, the greatest Czech player in history had a record-setting season that included 54

In 2005–2006 Jaromir Jagr had one of the greatest scoring seasons in Rangers history.

goals, a team record for a single campaign, and 69 assists, a number bested only by Brian Leetch (three times, with 80, 72, and 70), Sergei Zubov (77), and Wayne Gretzky and Mark Messier (72).

Jean Ratelle, 109

Ratty's production could have been even higher in the 1971–1972 season, but a broken ankle cost him the final 17 games. His 46 goals place him seventh on the single-season scoring list, and his playmaking (63 assists) was peerless. His left wing, Vic Hadfield, scored 50 that season, and right wing Rod Gilbert netted 43.

Mark Messier, 107

In his first season with the Rangers (1991–1992) after winning five Stanley Cups in Edmonton, Mess dished out 72 assists and scored 35 goals. On his first night, he set up Doug Weight for a goal in Montreal and kept rolling. He won the Hart Trophy as MVP as he led the team in points and to the Presidents' Trophy for the most points by a team.

Vic Hadfield, 106

The 1971–1972 season was a career year for the Ontario-born left winger, becoming the first Ranger to score 50 or more goals. The amazing sidebar was his 56 assists. After all, Hadfield was better known as an bruising enforcer, who had led the league in penalty minutes (157) in 1963–1964. He credited a Bobby Hull–style curved stick for his transition to a scorer, but he never really altered his rugged style. He had 142 penalty minutes in 1971–1972, which makes the 106-point figure even more remarkable. No player has figured out how to score from the sin bin!

Mike Rogers, 103

The speedy and prolific center came to the Rangers on October 2, 1981, in a trade with the Hartford Whalers for Chris Kotsopoulos, Gerry McDonald, and Doug Sulliman. The 5′9″ Rogers had scored 105 points in each of the previous two seasons and just about matched that number on Broadway in his first campaign with 65 assists and 38 goals. He became the third Ranger to crack the 100-point mark (after Ratelle and Hadfield). His 16-game point streak stood for 10 years before being snapped by Brian Leetch.

Brian Leetch, 102

In 1991–1992 the popular defenseman's productivity went through the Garden's circular roof. The 102 points (and the 80 assists) are the most by a Rangers defenseman in a single season.

Brian Leetch skips over Islanders defender Mathieu Schneider in a 1995 game. Leetch retired after an 18-year career in 2007.

He had 23 assists, including at least one in every game, in a record streak of 15 games from November 29 to December 31, 1991, and had five goals and 24 assists in setting the record for longest game streak for points—17 games—from November 23 to December 31, 1991.

NO. 99

Before the greatest player ever to play in the NHL retired, No. 99 had three wonderful years with the Rangers. Wayne Gretzky gave New York hockey fans a thrill.

After signing as a free agent in July 1996, the Great One—along with former Edmonton sidekick Mark Messier—carried the Rangers to the Eastern Conference Finals in his first season, only to lose to the Flyers.

Gretzky posted 97 points (25 goals and 72 assists) and almost duplicated that feat in 1997–1998, when he scored 23 goals and added 67 assists on Broadway without Messier, who had departed for Vancouver.

In 1998–1999 Gretzky, then 37, played just 70 games and had a career-low nine goals to go with 53 assists.

Although he was embraced by most Rangers fans, Gretzky rarely made the back pages of the New York papers in a city consumed by baseball, especially when the Mets and Yankees were winning.

The low-key Gretzky didn't have the brashness or the ego of a New York athlete–turned–power broker. Even at his last practice, he took things in stride.

As the drills wound down, Rangers coach John Muckler gathered the team and ordered that Gretzky skate some more.

"He told me to do a couple extra down and backs," Gretzky told reporters afterward. "I said, 'No, I'll retire right here.'" He went to center ice and led the stretching.

The final game of his incomparable career was a 2–1 overtime loss to the Penguins at Madison Square Garden on April 18, 1999. Jaromir Jagr, later to be a Rangers captain, scored the game-winner for Pittsburgh. Gretzky's final point was an assist on a Brian

The Great One's time in New York was short, but sweet. Photo courtesy of Getty Images.

Leetch goal. Gretzky was named as the first, second, and third star of the game and retired after 20 years in the NHL, holding 61 league records.

13s: SCOFFING AT SUPERSTITION

Just five Rangers have worn the No. 13 jersey:

Jack Stoddard—In 1951, he was acquired in a trade with the Providence Reds for Jean-Paul Denis, Pat Egan, and Zellio Toppazzini. The right wing from Stoney Creek, Ontario, played 80 games from 1951 to 1953, scored 16 goals, and had 15 assists.

Bob Brooke—The Acton, Massachusetts, native became the first former Yale player to play in the NHL when he made his debut on March 9, 1984. The next day, the center-turned–right wing scored his first goal in Edmonton on a 50-foot slap shot that beat Grant Fuhr. He was the only Ranger to notch a hat trick during the 1985–1986 season (versus Toronto on November 20, 1985). His biggest moment as a Ranger came when he tallied the game-tying goal with 2:35 left in regulation and scored the winner at 2:40 of overtime to beat Washington 6–5 in Game 4 of 1986 Patrick Division Finals on April 23 at the Garden. The second goal tied the series at two, and the Rangers went on to win the next two games. He later played for the Stars and Devils.

Sergei Nemchinov—Chosen in the 12th round of the 1990 NHL Draft, the Moscow native—along with Alexei Kovalev—were the first Russian players to win the Stanley Cup, when the Rangers triumphed in 1994. In 1992, as a rookie, he scored 30 goals to help the Rangers capture the Presidents' Trophy for the most points. In the championship season, he had 22 goals and 27 assists. He was traded to Vancouver late in the 1996–1997 season, eventually came back to the New York area, and is one of a handful of players to skate for all three metro-area teams, the Rangers, Islanders, and Devils.

Valeri Kamensky—The most skilled player of the five. A superb passer and effortless skater. Lethal slap shot. He came to the Rangers late in his career, at the age of 33, after winning the Cup with the Colorado Avalanche in 1996, when he posted his best numbers—38 goals and 47 assists—and was one of the top left wingers in the league. He spent two seasons in Manhattan, from 1999 to 2001, registering 27 goals and 39 assists.

Richard Scott—A brawler who amassed 28 major penalties (second in the AHL for one season) and had zero points in 10 games in 2001–2002. The right wing from Hawkestone, Ontario, is easily the most obscure of the No. 13 jersey-wearers.

A TALE OF TWO ULFS

Most rabid Rangers fans would recognize Ulf Nilsson, the Swedish star who fled the old World Hockey Association with Anders Hedberg in the summer of 1978 to join the Blueshirts.

Nilsson, who scored 57 goals and recorded 112 assists and helped the Rangers to the Stanley Cup Finals in their last season in New York, wasn't the first Swede to play for the club, as is commonly misreported.

That was another Ulf: Ulf Sterner.

Sterner wasn't just the first Swede to play on Broadway, he was the first European-born-and-bred player in the NHL. Sterner, a 23-year-old left wing, played four games in 1964 before returning home. A star in his Nordic homeland, he was physically and psychologically hammered by the abuse from the Canadian players, who dominated the league at the time.

Actually, the two Ulfs played together in Sweden in 1973.

And the pair had another link: Freddie "the Fog" Shero.

Shero was Sterner's first U.S. coach, with the Baltimore Clippers, a Rangers affiliate.

Shero also coached Nilsson in 1979.

MR. DURABLE

He came from all places, the Montreal Maroons, in December 1934.

And he became the Rangers' first regular goalie, because of his, well, regularity.

In the team's first 10 seasons, the club's goaltending was like a carousel: Hal Winkler, Lorne Chabot, and John Ross Roach all took turns in the cage, bouncing around like a loose puck on warming ice.

But David Alexander Kerr just wouldn't leave the crease.

For seven seasons, Kerr missed very, very, very few games. His missed 11 in 1934–1935, one in 1935–1936, and none, zero, nada, in the next five seasons. The apex? Playing all 48 regular-season games in the 1940 championship season and 12 in the Stanley Cup play-offs. He had an NHL-leading eight shutouts, a micro-scopic 1.54 goals-against average, and eight playoff victories.

Before weight training became a staple in dressing rooms and conditioning was demanded by coaching staffs, what impressed Kerr's peers was his endurance.

"He was always in fan-tastic shape and was really an inspiration for the other fellows to stay in shape," coach Frank Boucher once said.

THE MYSTERIOUS RANGERS

In the 1999 film *Mystery, Alaska*, a *Sports Illustrated* writer describes the Saturday night hockey games in this tiny burg, and the NHL arranges to send the Rangers north for a game against the town's team. Here's the fictional Rangers roster:

- 11 Jackson
- 44 Kangarpool
- 36 Robertson
- 16 Rory
- 19 LaViolette
- 22 Wasson
- 70 Neskoranty
- 55 Muldoon
- 41 Vogel
- 13 Yeaton
- 10 Kocreka
- 4 Coleman
- 34 Gaynor

MR. DURABLE II

Andy Hebenton played 560 consecutive games for the Blueshirts, plus 22 more in the Stanley Cup playoffs. The 582-game streak stands as the Rangers' all-time record, surpassing by 19 the team's first Iron Man, Murray Murdoch. Hebenton averaged more than 20 goals a season, scoring 177 times in eight years, and was a solid defensive forward and penalty-killer as well.

In June 1963 the Bruins claimed Hebenton in the Intra-League Draft. He played one season for the Bruins—all 70 games, naturally—before returning to the Western Hockey League, where he finished his professional career in 1975. Hebenton played 1,062 games as a pro without missing one. It was the death of his father that finally snapped the streak on October 18, 1967.

HAIL TO THE CHIEF

He was undoubtedly the greatest Ranger of Cree Indian heritage: James Anthony Neilson, No. 15. A solid defenseman for 12 Rangers seasons, only three backliners (Harry Howell, Ron Greschner, and Brian Leetch) have played more games for the Rangers.

At 6'2", 205 pounds, "the Chief" was a formidable but agile figure who was often used on left wing. In fact, it was on the flank where Neilson scored his first NHL goal at Boston Garden against the Bruins in the 1962–1963 season.

MANAGEMENT

HEAD COACHES, FROM BAD TO WORSE

In 81 years, the Rangers have had 35 different head coaches.

Doesn't say much for longevity behind the bench, does it?

And with only four Stanley Cups in those decades, well, it's easy to see why there's a swinging door on the bench.

Only 12 coaches have winning records, and some were very short stays: Lester Patrick (281–216–107); Phil Esposito (24–21–0, in two stints); Bernie Geoffrion (22–18–3); Emile Francis (342–209–103, in three stints); Larry Popein (18–14–9); Fred Shero (82–74–24); Herb Brooks (131–113–41); Michel Bergeron (73–67–18); Roger Neilson (141–104–35); Mike Keenan (52–24–8); Colin Campbell (118–108–43); and Tom Renney (133–98–35 through the 2007–2008 season). Note: the last category is ties or overtime losses.

Lester Patrick (1926–1927 to 1938–1939) was at the helm for two Stanley Cups; Frank Boucher one (1939–1940 to December 1948); and Mike Keenan one (April 1993 to July 1994).

Oh, there were droughts.

From 1943 to 1947, again in 1949, and then from 1951 through 1955, the Rangers missed the playoffs.

From 1959 to 1966, the Rangers were in the postseason just once: 1962, when they fell in the semifinals to Toronto, 4–2.

From 1967 to 1975, the Rangers qualified for the postseason every year. After missing in 1976 and 1977, they reeled off 10 consecutive seasons in the playoffs before falling short in 1988.

From 1989 to 1992, they qualified every year, missed the cut in 1993, and then won the Cup in 1994.

After advancing to the Eastern Conference Semifinals in 1995 and 1996, and the Conference Finals in 1997, a seven-year string of futility ensued.

In the 2005–2006 season, the year after the lockout, the Rangers qualified but were swept by the Devils, then made it to the conference semifinals in 2006–2007.

Some of the good, bad, and ugly among the coaches:

To be sure, Emile "the Cat" Francis stands above all the rest.

Francis, a former goaltender who backed up Chuck Rayner when the Rangers went to the Finals in 1950, found his rightful place in hockey in the front office and behind the bench. Francis's tenure lasted from 1965 to 1975, and the team made the playoffs for nine consecutive seasons.

The Cat holds the records for most games coached (654), wins (342), winning percentage (.602), playoff games (75), and playoff wins (34). He assembled the G-A-G Line, the Bulldog Line, and the combination of Ed Giacomin and Gilles Villemure, who shared the Vezina Trophy in 1970–1971.

Francis engineered the Rangers' run to the Finals in 1971–1972 and was devastated when they lost.

"We were right there, but we couldn't do it," he said years later. "The greatest disappointment of my career was not winning a Stanley Cup for the fans of New York. That's why I was so happy to be there when they finally did win it in 1994. I'll never forget that."

The era of Bryan Watson, who coached for three-plus seasons starting in 1955–1956, was notable for its wackiness. He battled constantly with his players, especially goaltender Gump Worsley, whom Watson always thought to be out of shape. Despite the hubbub, the Rangers made the playoffs for three consecutive years.

Perhaps the epitome of the Watson-era follies occurred on February 15, 1959, following a 5–1 loss to the Canadiens. He ordered the entire team—except for Worsley—back on the ice for a grueling postgame practice of skating drills without pucks. Many players said the practice destroyed the Rangers physically and psychologically, and the Rangers missed the playoffs on the final night of the season. Watson was replaced by another former player, Alf Pike, in November 1959. In 123 games, Pike's charges went 36-66-21.

Fred "the Fog" Shero, who led the Philadelphia Flyers to Stanley Cups in 1974 and 1975, coached in New York from June 1978 to November 1980. Shero, sometimes lost in thought, was a cerebral motivator, dishing out anecdotes and quotes like assists.

> "ALL I KNOW IS THAT WHEN I DIE, WHETHER I GO TO HEAVEN OR HELL, I'LL HAVE TO CHANGE AT JAMAICA."
> —BOOM BOOM GEOFFRION, WHO COMMUTED TO THE GARDEN ON THE LONG ISLAND RAILROAD, WITH ITS FAMOUS SWITCHING HUB IN QUEENS

Among my favorites: "Commitment is like ham and eggs. The chicken makes a contribution. The pig makes a commitment"; "Success is not the result of spontaneous combustion. You must first set yourself on fire"; "Fame is a vapor. Popularity an accident. Riches take wings. Only one thing endures, and that is character."

Herb Brooks—the Olympic coach who authored the "Miracle on Ice"—became the fastest coach in Rangers' team history to win 100 games, led the club to the playoffs in three of his four seasons (1981–1982, 1982–1983, 1983–1984), and lost each year to the Islanders. He was replaced by Ted Sator.

Sator guided the Rangers to the playoffs in 1985–1986 and advanced to the conference finals after beating Philadelphia and Washington, but lost in five to Montreal. The bloom was quickly off the budding flower, however. In 1986–1987 Sator was fired after a horrible start (5–12–6).

Colin Campbell, currently the NHL's czar of discipline (officially, the director of hockey operations and senior vice president), served three and a half years after Keenan was dismissed, and in his tenure, the Rangers made the postseason in 1994–1995, 1995–1996, and 1996–1997, making it to the conference finals that last season, only to lose to the Flyers.

Coach Jean-Guy Talbot (left) takes questions with GM John Ferguson during a press conference in August 1977.

Phil Esposito, the legendary scorer and Hall of Famer who spent most of his career with the Bruins, was coach and general manager from the 1975–1976 season to the 1980–1981 campaign. Known as "Trader Phil" for the flurry of swaps he made, including sending a first-rounder to the Quebec Nordiques for coach Marcel Bergeron. The high point of Espo's tenure was leading the Rangers to the Finals in 1979.

"Iron Mike" Keenan won the Cup in 1993–1994, but resigned in a power struggle with GM Neil Smith.

Roger Neilsen, known as "Captain Video" for his late-night devotion to watching and analyzing tape of opponents, won the Presidents Trophy in 1992.

Craig Patrick, the son of former player Lynn Patrick, was only a coach for parts of the 1980–1981 and 1984–1984 seasons. But his role in Rangers history came as Penguins general manager. He drafted Jaromir Jagr, then an unknown from Czechoslovakia, fifth overall in 1990. Years later, in 2001, he sent Jagr to the Caps, not the Rangers, because he demanded too much in return—reportedly Petr Nedved, Radek Dvorak, Mike York, and two prospects.

The biggest error was offering a job to former Islander star Bryan Trottier, who wowed general manager Glen Sather with a 40-page, handwritten response to a nine-page questionnaire about the team and what he would bring to the table in 2002.

But something was lost in translation. Trottier went 21–27–6 and was fired after 54 games.

Jean-Guy Talbot (August 1977 to June 1978) wore a warm-up outfit behind the bench rather than the traditional business suit. Former player Dave Maloney recalled Talbot, who spoke with a heavy accent, leaving the locker room laughing one night before a game in Toronto when Ron Low was the goaltender. "Jean-Guy could not quite get it out whether we should 'shoot high on dat guy Low or low on dat guy High.'" Talbot also wasn't the best at math. One time, unhappy with the offense, he said that each of the 17 players should have two shots on goal. "Dat way we have 37."

In one sense, Talbot helped start a player on his way to one of the finest coaching careers.

In a junior league game in March 1952, Talbot hit Scotty Bowman in the head with his stick. Bowman said afterward that he had headaches and blurred vision and "never had the same confidence" after the incident. He eventually became a minor-league coach and went on to become the winningest coach in NHL history.

From player to coach to player to coach. That's the story of the Boomer.

Emile Francis lured one of hockey's most storied names—Bernie "Boom Boom" Geoffrion—a skilled right winger who won six Stanley Cups in Montreal, to New York for a comeback after two years of coaching in the American Hockey League. Geoffrion's play helped the Rangers to the 1966–1967 playoffs for the first time in five seasons. But Geoffrion's comeback was hampered by injuries, so Francis named him coach, the 12th in club history, in the 1968–1969 season. Halfway through the season, suffering severe stomach problems, he stepped down.

The shortest tenure without illness? John Tortorella, winless in four games, replacing John Muckler at the end of the 2000 season.

OWNERS AND BOSSES

Some were hated, some were tolerated, all were corporations.

Since 1972 Madison Square Garden, and therefore the Rangers, has been a subsidiary of a larger, faceless corporation. From 1972 to 1989, it was owned by Gulf + Western (because of its sheer size, kiddingly called "Engulf and Western" by insiders). In 1989 it was renamed Paramount, which sold the Garden to Viacom Inc. in 1994. Soon afterward, Cablevision Systems became a part owner and later took full control.

Naturally, the front-office executives running the Rangers have been a business-oriented lot.

In the 1970s there was Alan N. Cohen, who said he would rather make a profit than win the Stanley Cup. His nickname? "Bottom Line."

Another colorful character was music company impresario and former owner of the Joe Namath–era Jets, Sonny Werblin, who ran the Garden from 1978 to 1984.

When he took over, both the Knicks and Rangers were sinking into the hole that started to be dug in the mid-1970s. He fired both Rangers general manager John Ferguson and coach Jean-Guy Talbot in June 1978, named Fred Shero as general manager, and spent money to acquire big names, such as defenseman Barry Beck.

Werblin also gets the credit for hiring—and firing—Herb Brooks, who directed the 1980 "Miracle on Ice" U.S. Olympic gold-medal team. For three years, Brooks and his "Smurfs"—the small, speedy players who embraced European-style, puck-possession hockey, took the Rangers to the playoffs, only to be knocked out by the Islanders, who were in their championship drives.

After Brooks publicly criticized Beck, calling him a "coward," both the defenseman and the team lost traction, and Werblin axed him.

James L. Dolan, the current chairman of Madison Square Garden, is perhaps the most vilified owner in the team's history. The son of Cablevision founder Charles Dolan, James Dolan—who heads a rock and blues band called J.D. and the Straight Shots (perhaps a veiled reference to his former treatment for alcohol abuse)—is admittedly more a fan of basketball than of hockey, and shows up at Knicks games far more than at Rangers games.

Critics blame Dolan, sometimes unjustly, for the team's failure to make the playoffs for seven consecutive years. Dolan allowed general manager Glen Sather to spend millions of dollars on high-priced veterans who turned out to be busts—Eric Lindros and Pavel Bure among them.

Dolan also has been lambasted by fans for his blind loyalty to Sather, who won several Stanley Cups in Edmonton, but since 2000, had failed to direct the Rangers past the second round of the playoffs through the 2007–2008 season.

Lindros was plagued by six concussions that turned him from a crease-crasher to a perimeter player, and the former Philadelphia Flyers center missed the entire 2000–2001 season in part because of a contract dispute. Neither deterred Sather. The Rangers took a risk, swapping forwards Jan Hlavac and Pavel Brendl, defenseman Kim Johnsson, and a third-round draft pick for Lindros. Then Sather gave him a $38 million, four-year contract. Lindros scored 37 goals and added 36 assists in the 2001–2002 season, then disintegrated. He had 19 goals and 34 assists the following year and played just 39 games in 2003–2004, with 10 goals and 22 assists.

Perhaps the greatest two gaffes—besides general manager Emile Francis waiving veteran goaltender Ed Giacomin on Halloween night in 1975, only to see him claimed by Detroit and three days later beat the Rangers in an emotional night at Madison Square Garden and then, a week later, trading Jean Ratelle and Brad Park to Boston for Phil Esposito and Carol Vadnais—involved the bungled handling of stars Mark Messier and Brian Leetch.

In 1997, three years after "the guarantee" of a Game 6 Rangers victory over the Devils in the Eastern Conference Finals (and three goals to assure it) followed by the first Rangers Cup in 50 years, Messier wanted a three-year contract.

Both general manager Neil Smith and Garden president Dave Checketts balked. Checketts said the organization did not believe

Messier was worth $20 million for the next three years. "How long should we pay for that Cup?" Checketts asked. "He played six years and won one Cup. We made a financial decision."

Messier left for Vancouver, saying, "I told them I would have taken less than that." The Rangers still had Wayne Gretzky and made an offer sheet to restricted free agent Joe Sakic, which the Colorado Avalanche matched. Gretzky retired the following year. Oops.

In his 17-year NHL career, Leetch played only with the Rangers, but in 2004 he was shipped to the Maple Leafs as the struggling Rangers, who were about to miss the playoffs for the seventh straight season, cleaned house.

The problem was that Leetch, a two-time Norris Trophy winner as the NHL's top defenseman and the last link to the Cup season, was never told about the deal before it was made, on his 36th birthday, and it left him bitter and fans outraged. The Rangers acquired defenseman Maxim Kondratiev, forward Jarkko Immonen, a first-round pick, and a second-round draft choice. The "Fire Sather" chants rang through the Garden, and Leetch was never forgotten.

THE BEST DRAFTS

In the waning rounds of a draft, some uncut gems are available. The right prospectors can mine them. In numerous years, the Rangers sifted through the possibilities and came up with some nuggets. They ranged from serviceable to solid to stars. Many, unfortunately, were traded and had fine careers with other teams.

1974—Ed Johnstone (104)

The popular little right wing from Brandon, Manitoba, played seven years with the Rangers, from 1975–1976 to 1982–1983, and scored 234 points in 371 regular-season games and 23 points in 53 playoff games. In 1981 he made the All-Star team and was voted team MVP. He was traded to Detroit with Ed Mio and Ron Duguay for Mike Blaisdell, Mark Osborne, and Willie "Baby" Huber on June 13, 1983, and retired in 1987.

Eddie Giacomin, shown here at the All-Star Game, was a fixture in the nets for the Rangers for eight seasons. Photo courtesy of Getty Images.

1978—Tom Laidlaw (93)
Former Islanders coach Al Arbour said the stay-at-home defenseman "just doesn't make mistakes," and the Rangers certainly didn't by picking the "Cowboy," who later became a player/agent.

THE TOP DRAFT PICKS

Longtime fans bemoan the busts in the first and second rounds of the Amateur Drafts since 1963.

No question, the Rangers could have fared better. There was no Mario Lemiuex, no Wayne Gretzky.

But there was Brian Leetch and Mike Richter, and for the most part—especially in the 1970s—the Rangers scored with their top picks in many years. Here are the players (their spot in the draft order); and the GM in charge:

1966: Defenseman Brad Park (2); Emile Francis
1971: Forward Steve Vickers (10); Francis
1973: Forward Rick Middleton (14), Pat Hickey (30); Francis
1974: Defensemen Dave Maloney (14), Ron Greschner (32); Francis
1976: Forward Don Murdoch (6); John Ferguson
1977: Forwards Lucien Deblois (8), Ron Duguay (13); Ferguson
1978: Forward Don Maloney (26); Fred Shero
1981: Defenseman James Patrick (9); Craig Patrick
1985: Goaltender Mike Richter (28); Patrick
1986: Defenseman Brian Leetch (9); Phil Esposito
1990: Center Doug Weight (34); Neil Smith
1991: Forward Alex Kovalev (15); Smith
1994: Goaltender Dan Cloutier (26); Smith
2001: Goaltender Dan Blackburn (10), defenseman Fedor Tyutin (40); Glen Sather

Laidlaw appeared in 510 games for the Blueshirts from 1980–1981 to 1986–1987 before a trade to Los Angeles.

1980—Reijo Ruotsalainen (119)

A major late-round steal. The fluid Finn known as "Rexi," whom legendary coach Herb Brooks called the best skater in the NHL in the late 1980s, played for the Rangers from 1981–1982 to 1985–1986. The smallish son of a coach, Rexi was part of a multi-player deal to Edmonton in March 1987, where he won two

Stanley Cups with the Oilers in 1987 and 1990. As a Ranger, he played 389 games, scored 99 goals, and added 217 assists, approaching a point-a-game pace.

1982—Kelly Miller (183)
The energetic playmaker and checker from Detroit was another steal for the Rangers. He played close to 1,000 NHL games, but less than two full seasons with the Rangers. He was shipped to Washington in a regrettable deal for Bobby Carpenter in 1987 and became one of the Capitals' all-time greats over 13 seasons.

1982—Tony Granato (120)
His Rangers career wasn't long, but his impact was felt. The Illinois native scored 36 goals as a rookie in 1988–1989, a team record. In 1990, however, he was traded to Los Angeles with Tomas Sandstrom for Bernie Nicholls.

Granato later became head coach of the Colorado Avalanche.

1984—Kjell Samuelsson (119)
A defenseman with talent who was sent away as well, Samuelsson played just 39 games for New York.

He eventually made his way to Pittsburgh, where he won a Stanley Cup in 1992 with Mario Lemieux, who, by the way, was the number-one pick in the same draft.

1986—Darren Turcotte (114)
A Boston native, Turcotte led the Rangers in goals with 32 in 1989–1990, one of his six seasons in New York. He finished up on Broadway with 122 goals (an average of more than 20 a season) in 255 games, and six goals in 24 postseason games. In November 1993 the center was traded to Hartford with James Patrick for a package that included Steve Larmer and Nick Kypreos. Turcotte subsequently played for the Sharks, Blues, and Predators.

1990—Sergei Zubov (85)
Another great pick—a critical player on the 1994 Cup team, an All-Star–caliber defenseman, a power-play quarterback, and

Sergei Zubov is considered one of the Rangers' better draft picks in their history. Photo courtesy of Getty Images.

another player who the Rangers absurdly traded away far too soon. The Moscow-born defenseman, selected in the fifth round, led the Cup team in points with 89 but was traded at age 25 with Petr Nedved to the Penguins for Luc Robitaille and Ulf Samuelsson in August 1995. Management was critical of Zubov's defensive skills, but he later won another Cup in Dallas, where he played for more than 10 years.

1990—Sergei Nemchinov (244)

The Rangers hoped Nemchinov, a Russian center, would be able to come to the U.S., and he did, the following season, and scored 30 goals in 1991–1992. The 12th-rounder played six years in Rangers blue, appearing in 418 games (with 105 goals and 120 assists) and 52 playoff games (7 goals and 15 assists). Sarge was traded to Vancouver in March 1997 but eventually returned to the New York metro area and is one of a handful of players who skated for the Rangers, Islanders, and Devils.

1993—Todd Marchant (164)

Although he played just one game for the Rangers, the Buffalo native had the stuff to stick in the league. The speedy center was traded to Edmonton for Craig MacTavish in March 1994, but Marchant lasted nine years with the Oilers and eventually was

ADDING INJURY

The Rangers also had some unfortunate injuries that derailed the promising careers of high draft picks.

Dan Blackburn had a real chance to be a star. In 2001–2002 he became the fifth-youngest goaltender in NHL history and second-youngest in franchise history to appear in an NHL game (18 years, 143 days on October 10). When the Rangers beat Montreal five days later, Blackburn became the third-youngest goaltender in NHL history and second-youngest in Rangers history to record an NHL win. He made 18 consecutive starts from November 7 through December 14. But before the next training camp, he sustained nerve damage in his left shoulder and missed the entire season. Despite surgery in March 2004, the 6'1" Blackburn couldn't play at the NHL level again and retired in 2005 after straining the MCL in his left knee. He was just 22.

Stefan Cherneski, a right wing from Winnipeg who was selected 19th overall in 1997, suffered a fractured right patella in the minors and retired in November 1998.

claimed on waivers by the Anaheim Ducks, where he won the Cup that he missed out on in New York. Fact: with the Oilers he was one of the few players to play for a coach for whom he once was traded (MacTavish).

1994—Kim Johnsson (286)

The Swedish defenseman stayed in his home country for five years before making the club in 1999.

But he played 151 games on the Rangers' blue line, many with Brian Leetch, and had 11 goals and 36 assists before a trade to Philadelphia, where for four years, Johnsson was their best offensive-minded defenseman.

1995—Marc Savard (91)

The slick, playmaking center from Ottawa lasted just two years with New York, scoring 10 goals and adding 41 assists in 98 games. He was shipped out in a head-scratching trade in which the Rangers received Jan Hlavac and two picks that turned into prospects that never blossomed. Savard later had seven consecutive 20-goal seasons for Calgary, Atlanta, and Boston. Ouch.

1997—Johan Holmqvist (175)

The seventh-round pick from Sweden appeared in just four games in three seasons before being sent to Minnesota in March 2003 for Lawrence Nycholat. The tall goaltender played in 2006–2007 with Tampa.

2000—Henrik Lundqvist (205)

Perhaps the Rangers' best eighth-round selection. The dazzling Swedish goaltender was a Vezina Trophy finalist in each of his first two years with the team and helped Sweden to the gold medal in the 2006 Winter Olympics. In 2006–2007 Lundqvist appeared in 70 games, posting a 37–22–8 record, a 2.34 goals-against average, a .917 save percentage, and five shutouts, as the Rangers advanced to the Eastern Conference Semifinals.

2002—Petr Prucha (240)

Perhaps the Rangers' second-best eighth-round selection. The swift, resilient Czech youngster scored 52 goals in his first two seasons in New York. In 2005–2006 his 16 goals on the power play usurped Camille Henry's total for a Rangers rookie.

THE RIVALRIES

AMERICANS

Decades before the on-ice tong wars between the Rangers and Islanders, the Rangers and Flyers, and the Rangers and Bruins, a pitched 15-year battle was waged in Manhattan.

Imagine the rivalry between a younger and older brother living in the same room of the family house, vying for attention, fighting to establish territory.

From 1927 to 1942, that summarized the intensity of the clashes between the New York Americans and the Rangers, bitter teams who shared the ice at Madison Square Garden.

"When we played each other, it was like a civil war," said Murray "Muzz" Patrick, who played in 16 games against the Amerks as a Ranger. "The landlords against the tenants. The aristocrats against the people's choice."

The Amerks rented the Garden first, in 1925, but when boxing promoter George Lewis "Tex" Rickard founded the Rangers in May 1926, he moved them into the building on 50th Street, as well.

The Rangers had won the Cup in 1928 and earned a playoff berth for nine consecutive years; the Americans were the second sibling, the blue collar to the Rangers' cufflinks.

New York's hockey community was divided, as well; when the teams faced each other, the seats were hard to come by, and the raucous house split by opposing cheers.

The game at the height of the rivalry between the two—and one that decided the winner of the first round of the Stanley Cup playoffs—started at 8:30 PM on March 27, 1938, and ended in the early morning hours of March 28.

According to the records, the game lasted 120:40—the length of two regular games—and ended at 1:30 in the morning. It remains the longest game ever played at any of the four Madison Square Gardens.

In the fourth overtime, the Amerks' Lorne Carr, a swift little right wing who earned the nickname "Sudden Death" after this marathon, beat Rangers goalie Davey Kerr for the 3–2 win. The resulting story marked the first time that a hockey game made the front page of *The New York Times*.

The Chicago Blackhawks silenced the Amerks in the next round, and in the ensuing years, as the Rangers' payroll and ability to land star players—and thus their popularity—grew, the little brother's fan base shrunk. In 1941, hoping to capitalize on the success of the Brooklyn Dodgers, owner Mervyn "Red" Dutton changed the club's name to the Brooklyn Americans—and staged practices in the borough—to no avail. The NHL assumed control of the foundering franchise and shuttered it in 1942.

ISLANDERS

The rivalry with suburban New York ties was clearly the one that still makes the blood of fans boil in the Nassau Coliseum and the Garden, in bars, and most recently, on Internet message boards, where profane vitriol flies through the ether before and after every game.

In 1978–1979 the Islanders collected 51 wins and a league-high 116 points, and swept the first round of the playoffs. In the semifinals, however, they met the Rangers, and the series pulled in even non–hockey fans. The tradition of the Rangers versus the upstart, six-year-old, expansion Isles. Suburbs against city, Seventh Avenue versus Hempstead Turnpike.

Another juxtaposition: Ron Duguay and his celeb teammates filmed commercials for tight-fitting Sasson jeans; the Isles' gritty

As this battle from April 2008 demonstrates, the bad blood between the Rangers and Islanders continues to this day. Photo courtesy of Getty Images.

defenseman Denis Potvin used muscle to make his point. Rangers goalie John Davidson was a stud, and a defensive scheme stifled Islander sharpshooters Mike Bossy, Bryan Trottier, and Clark Gillies by banging Potvin relentlessly. The Blueshirts won in six games.

"We turned up our intensity three notches in those playoffs," Davidson explained. "We eliminated Potvin whenever he carried the puck and never let him get back into the play."

Said Gillies, "I give Davidson all the credit. After it was over, we asked ourselves, 'What do we need to do to keep from folding?' We decided to pace ourselves during the regular season. The next year we finished second but won it all. Nobody remembers you finishing first if you don't win the Cup."

For four straight seasons, from 1980 to 1983, the Islanders did just that: they were Stanley Cup champions and erased the Rangers each year in the playoffs.

In 1980–1981 the Rangers had beaten the Kings and Blues in the first two rounds. But the Isles swept the Rangers, coached by Craig Patrick, 5–2, 7–3, 5–1, and 5–2, to win their second of four Cups. "They were just too good for us," Ulf Nilsson said. "To be successful, you have to have the best role players...that's what they had."

FLYERS

The Broad Street Bullies were the hated rivals in the 1970s. One series provided a microcosm for the rivalry.

In 1973–1974 the Rangers finished in third place in the East Division with a 40–24–14 record and upset the second-place Canadiens in six games in the first round. First-place Philadelphia beckoned.

The Rangers had All-Star defenseman Brad Park, who scored 25 goals and a remarkable 57 assists. They had the Goal-a-Game (G-A-G) Line in Vic Hadfield, Jean Ratelle, and Rod Gilbert; the Bulldogs in Steve Vickers, Walt Tkaczuk, and Bill Fairbairn; and a third line of Ted Irvine, Pete Stemkowski, and Bruce MacGregor.

But the Flyers had enforcer Dave "the Hammer" Schultz, and the Rangers wilted.

"[Coach] Emile Francis didn't believe in that," Stemkowski would recall. "We were a little intimidated...Park would go [fight], Ron Harris would. But we didn't have that killer."

At the Spectrum in Philadelphia, the Flyers won Games 1 and 2, then the Rangers tied the series, winning 3 and 4 at the Garden, with Gilbert ending Game 4 just 4:20 into overtime. The Flyers won Game 5 in Philadelphia, 4–1. The Rangers won Game 6 in New York, 4–1.

In that critical Game 7, with blood-lust reigning at the Spectrum, the game was scoreless, and at 11:55 Schultz mercilessly beat up Rangers defenseman Dale Rolfe. No one responded. "Hadfield couldn't fight because he broke his thumb in the last game of the regular season," Francis said. "And Ron Harris wasn't on the ice."

"That was the absolute key," former Flyers center Bill Clement said. "Schultz not only took him down but took his team down with him."

Not quite. Fairbairn gave the Rangers a 1–0 lead at 13:43. But Philadelphia's Rick MacLeish, Orest Kindrachuk, and Gary Dornhoefer scored to take a 3–1 into the third period. Vickers and Stemkowski scored for the Blueshirts in the third, but Dornhoefer scored another for Philly, and the Rangers scrambled into the closing minutes but fell 4–3. The Flyers then beat Boston to win their first of two Cups.

DEVILS

In the 2007–2008 season, the New Jersey Devils moved from their arena in East Rutherford to a $350 million palace in Newark.

The Rangers were happy to bid farewell to the arena off Exit 16W of the New Jersey Turnpike known as "the Swamp," which often mired the Rangers in the regular season.

The Devils' first-ever victory at home, October 8, 1982, was a 6–5 triumph over Herb Brooks's Rangers, and since they moved from Denver in 1982–1983, the Devils were 44–25–41 against the Rangers at the Meadowlands en route to winning three Stanley Cups, in 1995 (after the Rangers' victory in 1994), 2000, and 2003. Defenseman Scott Stevens constantly battled Rangers center Mark Messier (the two would be inducted into the Hall of Fame together in 2007). The Rangers' sweetest moment came in ousting the Devils from the postseason in the second round in 1997.

And as a final playoff farewell, the Devils dispatched the 2005–2006 Rangers with a humiliating four-game sweep in the first round. It was the first time they had topped the Rangers in a playoff series.

WHAT'S IN A NAME?

THE LINES

The A-Line. The Bread Line. The G-A-G Line. The Bulldog Lines. The Godfather and Two Dons. The Powerhouse Line. The Old Smoothies.

In most sports, individuals or teams have nicknames.

Almost every player in hockey has some sort of nickname—ranging from the simplest (adding a *y* or *ie* to *Jones* or *Smith*)—to the far more colorful.

Rangers center Alf Pike, for example, a rookie in the team's 1939–1940 Cup championship year, was known as "the Embalmer." Pike didn't preserve leads: he was a mortician in the off-season.

Yet the fans and the newspaper scribes usually bestowed one unit—the forward line—with the most memorable monikers.

For the Rangers, the first line to have a title was the formidable trio of left wing Bill Cook, center Frank Boucher, and right wing Fred "Bun" Cook.

They were the A-Line, named for the subway that rumbled underground north and south on Eighth Avenue through the city, and under the Garden, the A Train.

Bill and Fred, eight years Bill's junior, were the foundation of the Rangers. While playing for the Saskatoon Crescents, Conn Smythe—the first general manager of the franchise—signed the brothers. They persuaded Smythe to sign Boucher, whom they had played against. They debuted in the 1926–1927 season and developed what is now known as "chemistry."

Said broadcaster Foster Hewitt, the line "played like they had the puck on a string."

Indeed, according to Frank Selke, writing in *Legends of Hockey*: "The Cook-Boucher line introduced a style of attack completely their own—each member kept working into an open spot, passing the puck carefully and adequately, and frequently pushing the puck into the open net after confusing the defensive force of the opposition. This was a repetition of lacrosse as played by the great Indian teams."

One of their weapons: the previously unseen drop pass. "I had a dream about the drop pass one night, and at our next practice, I told Frank and Bill about it," Bun once recalled. "They thought I was crazy, but they decided to humor me. By gosh, it worked! I'd cross over from left wing to center as I moved in on defense. I'd fake a shot and leave the puck behind and skate away from it, with Frank or Bill picking it up. We got a lot of goals off the criss-cross and drop pass."

All three would eventually be inducted into the Hall of Fame, the only Rangers line to do so.

In the 1936–1937 season, another line starring two brothers was a staple: the Bread Line. It was hardly stale. In fact, with left wing Alex Shibicky, 22, center Ned Colville, 22, and right wing Mac Colville, 20, it was the youngest in the league.

Sportswriters didn't endow the trio with the name for the queues of the poor waiting for food outside churches. No, the Colvilles and Shibicky were the team's core, its "bread and butter."

All three players were from Western Canada and also were called "the Prairie Boys."

Shibicky contended that he was the first player to unleash a slap shot in an NHL game. "I learned it from Bun Cook [who was his roommate in 1935–1936]," Shibicky said, "but he only used it in practice. I was the first to use it in a game."

Perhaps the most famous line in team history, the G-A-G (Goal-a-Game) Line led the Rangers of the late 1960s and early 1970s.

The name for the threesome of left wing Vic Hadfield, silky center Jean Ratelle, and right wing Rod Gilbert was concocted by team statistician Arthur Friedman. Ratelle and Gilbert were long-time mates from juniors in Canada, and when Emile Francis added Hadfield, the trio took off.

In 1971–1972, with Hadfield as team captain, the line—which Friedman also dubbed the T-A-G Line (during a streak of two goals a game)—were ranked one, two, and three in team scoring. With two goals in the final game of the season against the Canadiens at Madison Square Garden, Hadfield became the team's first 50-goal scorer and, at the time, only the sixth player in the NHL to net half a hundred.

Gilbert, with the most goals (406), and Ratelle (second with 336) rank number one and number three on the team's all-time scoring list with 1,021 and 981 points. Hadfield is ninth in points with 572, and fifth in goals with 262.

There were actually two Bulldog Lines, known not solely for their bite, but for their bark—their defensive tenacity. Walt Tkaczuk centered both of the trios, and Billy Fairbairn was the right wing. Dave Balon was the original left wing. When Balon was traded to Vancouver in 1971, Steve Vickers took his spot, and the Bulldogs barked again.

Tkaczuk, a teenage worker in a gold mine in South Porcupine, Ontario, used to carry dynamite to older miners, and, the story goes, when he was identified as a top prospect with the Kitchener Rangers, William Jennings, the Rangers' longtime president and governor asked, "If he's that great, shouldn't we get him a safer job?"

As a Ranger, Tkaczuk proved to be a man of different mettle, or metal—iron. In 14 years he played 945 games as a Blueshirt (only three other Rangers reached that pinnacle), missing the 1,000-game mark due to an eye injury in 1980–1981. In two of those years, 1972 and 1979, the team went to the Finals. He ranks sixth on the team's all-time scoring list with 678 points (227 goals and 451 assists).

Fairbairn, from Brandon, Manitoba, was another tenacious player who illustrated the concept of a classic two-way player: one who could contribute on the scoresheet but also check the other team's key players. He played seven full seasons in New York and scored 22 or more goals in four of them.

Balon became a Bulldog in his second campaign with the Rangers. He had been traded to Montreal with Gump Worsley, Leon Rochefort, and Len Ronson for Jacques Plante, Don Marshall, and Phil Goyette on June 4, 1963. When he returned via another trade, he blossomed, leading the team in goals with 33 in 1969–1970 and 36 in 1970–1971. With Balon, the line registered 203 points in 1969–1970, finishing ahead of the G-A-G Line in scoring.

After Balon departed, the Rangers tried 16 different left wings in an attempt to rekindle the flame with Tkaczuk and Fairbairn. Then came Sarge, as Vickers was known (for wearing an old Army shirt to practices) in 1972. Gene Carr was injured, and Vickers was penciled in on November 22, 1972, against Los Angeles. He went on to score 30 goals and win the Calder Trophy as rookie of the year.

Maybe it was some 1979 channeling of Martin Scorsese. Without a doubt, Phil Esposito was a Sinatra and Como guy, an Italian stallion who said his most painful moment in hockey was his trade from his beloved Boston to New York in 1976.

But in 1979 Esposito found new mates, left wing Don Maloney and right wing Don Murdoch. Hence: "the Godfather and Two Dons."

The rookie Maloney scored his first NHL goal on his very first shot on February 14, 1979, against those Bruins at the Garden, and the trio tore up the place from there, as the Rangers bolted to the Finals. Esposito, who had scored 76, 68, and 66 goals for the Bruins in the early 1970s, still had a presence in front of the net and notched 42. Maloney had just nine in the regular season but deposited seven goals and 13 assists in 18 playoff games, a team record.

Murdoch, who was suspended for 40 games following a cocaine and marijuana bust at an airport, scored 15 in 40 games. The line disintegrated, however, as Murdoch, the centerpiece of a hard-partying group that frequented Manhattan's Studio 54 and

With Don Maloney and Don Murdoch as his wingers, Phil Esposito centered one of the more memorable lines in Rangers history—"the Godfather and the two Dons." Photo courtesy of Getty Images.

included Ron Greschner and Ron Dougay, never reached his potential.

When the Rangers needed a jolt in the 1939–1940 championship season, they turned to the Powerhouse Line: left wing Lynn Patrick, center Phil Watson, and right wing Bryan Hextall. Together, they combined for 43 goals and 59 assists in that 48-game season.

Hextall, who led the NHL in scoring in 1941–1942 with 56 points, has family ties as well. His son, Bryan Jr., played 21 games for the Rangers in 1962–1963; his grandson, Ron, was a slick stick-handling Flyers goaltender who became the first netminder in the NHL to score a goal—into an empty net in the 1987–1988 season. On April 11, 1989, he scored the first goal by a goaltender in the Stanley Cup playoffs. Watson coached in the AHL and for the Bruins in the mid-1960s.

For most of his time in New York, Bob Nevin's veteran linemates were center Phil Goyette and left wing Donnie Marshall. They were the "the Old Smoothies." Nevin came to the Rangers from Toronto in a blockbuster trade in February 1964, in which Andy Bathgate was shipped to the Leafs. Another South Porcupine native, Nevin was a quality player, but never filled Bathgate's shoes. Captain for six years, Nevin led the Rangers in scoring in 1965–1966 and had a career high 31 goals in 1968–1969. Goyette and Marshall arrived from Montreal with Jacques Plante in the summer of 1963. Marshall, an elite penalty killer, had honed his defensive skills with the Canadiens, where he was part of five Cup-winning teams from 1956 to 1960. Goyette has a dubious distinction: he was the first head coach of the rival New York Islanders in the 1972–1973 season. He lasted 48 games.

TOP NICKNAMES: FROM CHING TO GUMP

Detroit had Sid "Old Bootnose" Abel. The Flyers had Ken "the Rat" Linseman. Toronto had "the Big M," Frank Mahovlich. Montreal had "the Rocket" and "Pocket Rocket," Maurice and Henri Richard. Chicago had Elmer "Moose" Vasko and Eric "Elbows" Nesterenko. Here are some of my favorite Rangers nicknames:

Ching

Ivan "Ching" Johnson, a bruising defenseman on the championship teams of 1927 and 1930, was hardly of Asian descent.

When he and his teammates and fishing buddies would trek to the Red River in Alberta during the summers, he would volunteer to cook—rather than—as was the common practice of the time—hire a man of Chinese heritage to prepare meals on the trip.

The name stuck, and at the Garden, fans would shout "Ching, Ching, Chinaman!" In 403 games, Johnson posted modest offensive numbers, (38 goals and 48 assists), but he struck fear into forwards, finishing with 798 penalty minutes. In 1958 he was elected to the Hall of Fame.

Never

He hailed from Antigonish, Nova Scotia, and battled his way up through juniors and the minors. Frank "Never" Beaton scored just one goal and one assist in 25 games as a Ranger from 1978 to 1980. The left winger's forte was throwing punches.

In 1978 the 5'10", 200-pounder accumulated 319 penalty minutes for the New Haven Nighthawks, the Rangers affiliate. In 1979 his brawl with Paul Stewart of the Quebec Nordiques had the Garden rocking. Later in his career, after he lost a few scraps, his nickname was changed: he was then referred to as Frank "Seldom" Beaton.

Gump

Lorne John Worsley was a true character, who graced the Garden stage and locker room from 1953 to 1963. But everybody knew the 5'7", courageous, crew-cut, quip-happy goalie as "Gump" or "the Gumper." Worsley, whose moniker came from the comic strip character Andy Gump, wore no face mask through 583 games for the Rangers and bore the scars of honor.

In those years, the Rangers defense was, shall we say, often transparent. He was team MVP in 1961 and 1963, when he often was strafed by opposing teams. The Montreal native called getting into the net "going into the barrel"—referring to shooting fish in a barrel—no escape from the barrage. One night he was asked

A BORN RANGER

During the waning rounds of the 1986 draft, in which the Rangers had selected Brian Leetch with their first choice, one player left on the board seemed intriguing.

And obvious.

So at number 198, when their turn came, the remaining Rangers personnel at the table—GM Phil Esposito had left—picked a defenseman with an appropriate moniker: Joe Ranger.

But Ranger, a 6', 225-pound defenseman from Sudbury, Ontario, never skated as a New York Ranger.

He did play one season, 1987–1988 with the Kitchener Rangers of the Ontario Hockey League.

Before that, he played two seasons with the Windsor Compuware Spitfires.

Wonder if there ever was a Joe Compuware...?

which team gave him the most agony, and he deadpanned: "the Rangers."

Worsley, who often feuded with coach Phil Watson, was traded to Montreal in 1963, where he won four Stanley Cups. He played 21 years total in the NHL and retired at age 44. Only in his last six games—as a Minnesota North Star in 1974—did he wear a mask.

Taffy
Clarence "Taffy" Abel. The big fella (6'1", 225 pounds) was one of the first U.S.-born players to play regularly in the NHL. Together with Ching Johnson—his partner on defense—they tipped the scales at about 428 pounds. Abel wasn't raised near the ocean (Sault Sainte Marie, Michigan) but loved salt-water taffy.

The Count, or Gratoony the Loony
Perhaps the oddest duck to wear a Rangers uniform was goaltender Gilles Gratton. Gratton, a Quebec native, was the first Rangers goalie to wear the birdcage-style mask. He played 41 games for the Rangers in the 1976–1977 season and was called

"the Count" and "Gratoony the Loony." Gratton, a classical pianist, believed in reincarnation. A persistent pain in his left side, he said, had been the result of a lance wound during the Inquisition. He also claimed that, as a Spanish count in a former life, he helped stone people to death. Too bad he didn't stone more shooters.

Camille the Eel

Cammy Henry, or "Camille the Eel," was 5'7" of slippery. For 12 years, the elusive left winger scooted and sniped and was perhaps the best power-play skater of his era when it came to deflecting and redirecting slap shots from the point into the cage.

> **"HE BRINGS SOMETHING SPECIAL. I DON'T KNOW WHAT IT IS, BUT IF YOU ASK HIM, YOU WOULDN'T UNDERSTAND HIS ANSWER."**
> —WAYNE GRETZKY ON MULTILINGUAL (OR MULTI-GIBBERAL) RANGERS FORWARD ESA TIKKANEN

From 1953 to 1968, Henry scored 256 goals and 222 assists, and, in his Calder Trophy–winning rookie year, scored four goals on March 13, 1954, against the great Terry Sawchuk in Detroit, a feat that was never duplicated against the goaltender in his stellar career.

The Grate One

Then there was Esa Tikkanen. The pest from Helsinki was appropriately called "the Grate One." Originally an Oiler, he played in Edmonton on a line with Wayne Gretzky, the legit "Great One." Tikkanen was a distracting yapper, whose often-colorful stream of linguistic taunting was a mix of Finnish, Swedish, English, and words he made up. He also scored 30 goals three times and won five Stanley Cups, including one with the Rangers in 1994. But his annoying patter was as funny as it was irritating—and indecipherable. "He brings something special. I don't know what it is, but if you ask him, you wouldn't understand his answer," said Gretzky. Former Rangers center and Oilers coach Craig MacTavish put it differently: "Esa talks twice as much as anybody else. That's because you can understand only half of what he says."

Devils right wing John MacLean is knocked down by Esa Tikkanen during the 1997 Eastern Conference Semifinals.

Honorable Mentions

He loved to talk, brought kielbasa on team flights, and was proud of his heritage. Pete Stemkowski was the fun-loving "Polish Prince."

Left wing Greg "Indiana" Polis arrived in New York after a swap with the St. Louis Blues for Larry Sacharuk in 1974.

Jim "the Chief" Neilson, of Ojibwa decent, patrolled the blue line from 1962 to 1974.

Other nicknames that were more than just a play on one's name that I'd be remiss not to include: Barry "Bubba" Beck, Art "the Trapper" Coulter, "Leapin' Lou" Fontinato, Emile "the Cat" Francis, "Hot Rod" Gilbert, Ed "Boxcar" Hospodar, Chris "Knuckles" Nilan, Alexander "Pottsy" Karpovtsev, and John "the Beezer" Vanbiesbrouck.

ALL-TIME RANGERS ROSTER

There are Rangers, and there are ultimate Rangers, men whose careers were defined by the intoxicating mix of the cool white ice and the superheated, demanding atmosphere of Madison Square Garden, indelibly colored by Broadway blue.

I have selected a personal Top 25—plus two coaches—men who performed in the clutch and whose names endure: good guys who ably represented the team and the city and whose efforts and talents helped shape an Original Six franchise through eight decades of the good, the bad, and the ugly.

The roster is open to debate; many worthy candidates and fan favorites mentioned elsewhere in this collection didn't make my squad. But I've crafted a battle-hardened group of winners, a team that honors both accomplishments and tradition, character and courage, leadership and legend, savvy and soul.

In alphabetical order, the forwards (12): Andy Bathgate, Frank Boucher, Bill Cook, Rod Gilbert, Adam Graves, Vic Hadfield, Anders Hedberg, Don Maloney, Mark Messier, Jean Ratelle, Walt Tkaczuk, and Steve Vickers.

The defensemen (6): Ron Greschner, Harry Howell, Brian Leetch, Ching Johnson, James Patrick, and Brad Park.

The goaltenders (4): Ed Giacomin, Dave Kerr, Mike Richter, and Gump Worsley. The reserves (3): Camille Henry, Andy Hebenton, Dave Maloney. The coaches: Emile Francis and Lester Patrick.

OFFENSE

Andy Bathgate

When the Red Wings and Canadiens dominated the division, and the Rangers struggled in the 1950s and early '60s, the right wing was a beacon in the twilight, landing on the scoresheet almost nightly. Between 1952–1953 and 1963–1964, the prolific Bathgate averaged more than a point a game: in 719 games, he had 272 goals, 457 assists, and 444 penalty minutes. In the 22 playoffs

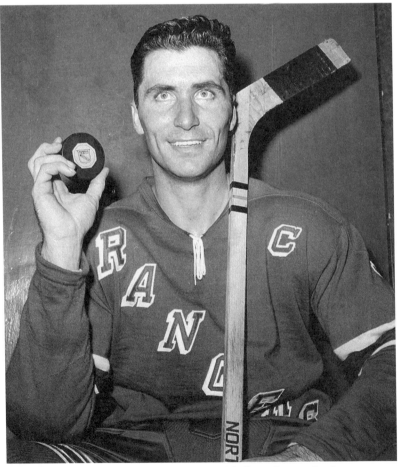

Andy Bathgate poses in the locker room at Madison Square Garden on November 12, 1961, after scoring the 200th goal of his career.

games during his tenure, the Winnipeg native, who was drafted by the Rangers, never missed a beat, with nine goals and seven assists. The four-time All-Star finished the 1961–1962 season tied with Bobby Hull in scoring with 84 points; Hull won the Art Ross Trophy by scoring 50 goals to Bathgate's 28, although Bathgate led the league with 56 assists. His successful third-period penalty shot against Detroit's Hank Bassen at the Garden on March 14, 1962—with nine days left in the season—not only won the game 3–2, but gave the Rangers a much-needed lift to help secure their first playoff spot in four years. The Rangers compiled just two winning campaigns in Bathgate's 12 years as a Ranger, but beginning in the 1955–1956 season, Bathgate finished in the top 10 in the NHL in scoring for nine straight years.

Frank Boucher
An original Ranger, Boucher recorded the franchise hat trick: he played center from 1926 to 1938, coached from 1939 to 1948, and was general manager from 1946 to 1955. On the ice, Boucher was the Wayne Gretzky of his era, a magical playmaker who led the Rangers to Stanley Cup championships in 1928 and 1933, and earned a reputation as one of the cleanest players in the sport. He won the NHL's Lady Byng Trophy seven times, after which the league gave the hardware to him permanently and had a new trophy crafted. Behind the bench, he guided the team to another Cup in 1940. Like Gretzky in Edmonton, Boucher was the recognizable face of the franchise in New York, and as a Rangers executive, he cofounded the Rangers Fan Club in 1950. His numbers: 413 points in 533 games (152 goals and 261 assists). He led the team in assists eight times and the league three times. Boucher, an Ottawa native, even came out of retirement for 15 games in the 1943–1944 season. He didn't lose his touch, netting four goals and 10 assists.

Bill Cook
The Rangers' first captain, William Osser Cook and his brother, Fred, known as "Bun," were Rangers who skated in the team's inaugural season of 1926–1927. Bill Cook was hardly a rookie; he

Frank Boucher, manager-coach of the Rangers, talks to members of the squad prior to their first workout at the Olympic Arena in Lake Placid, New York, in the late 1940s.

was 30 and scored the Blueshirts' first goal at 10:37 of the second period in a 1–0 opening night victory over the Montreal Maroons on November 16, 1926. The burly right wing, who wore No. 5, led the NHL in scoring during the Stanley Cup championship seasons of 1927 and 1933, was the first Ranger to win the Art Ross Trophy and to be voted an NHL first-team All-Star (in 1930–1931 and for the next two seasons). The Rangers line with Bun and Frank Boucher—who compared Bill to Rocket Richard and Gordie Howe—scored every goal in the Finals in 1927. In 12 seasons with the Rangers, the sharpshooter had 229 goals and 138 assists and was inducted into the Hall of Fame in 1952. Cook was ranked number 44 in a 1998 *Hockey News* list of the 100 top players in history. He later coached the Cleveland Barons and other teams, and died in 1986.

IN THE HALL

Forty-two men who played for the Rangers and eight executives are enshrined in the Hockey Hall of Fame in Toronto.

The players are: Howie Morenz, Lester Patrick, Bill Cook, Frank Boucher, Ching Johnson, Babe Siebert, Earl Siebert, Doug Bentley, Max Bentley, Babe Pratt, Neil Colville, Bryan Hextall, Bill Gadsby, Terry Sawchuk, Bernie Geoffrion, Doug Harvey, Chuck Rayner, Art Coulter, Johnny Bower, Tim Horton, Andy Bathgate, Jacques Plante, Harry Howell, Lynn Patrick, Gump Worsley, Allan Stanley, Rod Gilbert, Phil Esposito, Jean Ratelle, Ed Giacomin, Guy Lafleur, Buddy O'Connor, Brad Park, Clint Smith, Marcel Dionne, Edgar Laprade, Fred "Bun" Cook, Wayne Gretzky, Mike Gartner, Jari Kurri, Pat LaFontaine, and Dick Duff.

The others—known as builders—are: John Kilpatrick, William Jennings, Emile Francis, Bud Poile, Glen Sather, Craig Patrick, Roger Neilson, and Herb Brooks.

Waiting in the wings: Brian Leetch, Mike Richter, Jaromir Jagr, and Brendan Shanahan.

Rod Gilbert

Just imagine what a healthy Gilbert could have accomplished. In 18 years and 1,065 regular-season games with the Rangers, the French-Canadian right wing amassed 406 goals, 615 assists, and 1,021 points. He is the team's all-time leading goal-scorer and point-getter. In 79 playoff games, he mustered 34 goals and 67 points. From 1960 to 1978, he set or equaled 20 team scoring records. And he did it all with a reconstructed back. In juniors, he tripped over a cardboard lid from an ice-cream container during a home game and underwent spinal fusion. There were questions about whether he would ever play again. He did, and when opportunity knocked in the spring of 1962, Gilbert capitalized. During a playoff series against the Leafs, Ken Schinkel broke his toe. Then 20, Gilbert was summoned and scored two goals in his first game while playing on a line with Dave Balon and Johnny Wilson. His greatness blossomed with former childhood friend Jean Ratelle and Vic Hadfield on the G-A-G (Goal-a-Game) Line, especially in 1971–1972, when each player had more than 100 points and the Rangers went to the Finals, only to lose to the Bruins. Gilbert, elected to the Hall of Fame in 1982, skated for Team Canada when they defeated the Soviet Union team in the September 1972 Summit Series. "That was my Stanley Cup," he once said.

Adam Graves

The Toronto native was on the Kid Line with Joe Murphy and Martin Gelinas when the Edmonton Oilers won the Stanley Cup in 1990. After signing as a free agent with the Rangers in 1991, Adam Graves became a man whose generosity and willingness to donate time to charities and youth groups is unparalleled—and well-documented—and continues as a Rangers ambassador. On the ice, Graves made equal contributions as he transformed from a checking forward to a power forward who battled nightly in front of the net. In his 10 seasons in New York, he scored 22 goals or more in seven of them, 30 or more three times, and 10 in the magical Stanley Cup championship playoff run in 1994. During that season, Graves broke Vic Hadfield's record of 50 goals with 52. His 51st, fittingly, came against the Oilers in Edmonton. Jaromir Jagr would later break that mark, a feat Graves lauded with his characteristic humility. "I was never a guy that was looked upon as a points guy," Graves told *The New York Times* at the time. "I scored most of my goals within a 10-foot radius of the net, and they were ugly. That's the way I played." In the opinion of many fans, the No. 9 jersey—which both he and Bathgate wore—will appropriately be the next sweater to be retired.

Vic Hadfield

His was a Rangers career that exceeded expectations, and started, improbably, when he was waived by Chicago in 1961. Initially an enforcer—and practical joker in the locker room—who led the NHL with 151 penalty minutes in 1963–1964, Hadfield's scoring prowess boomed when paired with slick center Jean Ratelle and winger Rod Gilbert. "Jean and I needed somebody to go to the front of the net and hold his ground," Gilbert once told Stan

The Rangers' G-A-G Line of Vic Hadfield, Rod Gilbert, and Jean Ratelle move in on Bobby Orr and Ed Johnston during an early 1970s game against the Bruins. Photo courtesy of Getty Images.

Fischler. "Vic had a very short fuse. He was a tough guy, very robust. By being in front and yelling for the puck, Vic developed really good scoring skills." The Ontario native was the first Ranger to score 50 goals—with the last coming on a tap-in past Montreal's Denis DeJordy at the Garden—in 1971–1972, his first of three years as team captain. He also set a team record for power-play goals with 23. After 13 years, Hadfield ranked number nine on the Rangers all-time scoring list with 262 goals and 310 assists for 572 points in 839 games. And his 1,036 penalty minutes put him at number five in that category, as well.

Anders Hedberg

Although several European-born and -raised players had previously skated for the Rangers, Hedberg was the first such star. The Swedish great shone for the World Hockey Association's Winnipeg Jets, where both he and Ulf Nilsson played on a line with Bobby Hull, and Hedberg led the WHA with 70 goals in 1976–1977. The next summer, both Nilsson and Hedberg were enticed by Garden boss Sonny Werblin to sign with the Rangers for $2.4 million, and Hedberg scored 33 goals and added 45 assists as the Rangers went to the Finals. Hedberg was lost most of the 1982–1983 season with a knee injury. Yet in the six full seasons with the Rangers, the blond right wing always had at least 20 goals and 50 points. He ended up 17th on the all-time scoring list with 172 goals and 225 assists, and is the highest-scoring European in Rangers history. He won the Masterton Trophy in 1985, was a two-time All-Star, and Rangers MVP.

Don Maloney

An overnight success would be a fair way to describe the debut of Maloney, the team's first pick in the 1978 draft. The gritty left wing scored on his first NHL shot against the Bruins on February 14, 1979, against Gilles Gilbert and notched an assist on the next shift. If that wasn't quick enough, Maloney holds the record for the fastest three goals by one player in team history, notching the hat trick within a span of 2:30 on February 21, 1981, versus Washington at Madison Square Garden. As the Rangers surged to the Stanley Cup Finals in his rookie season, Maloney scored seven goals and posted 13 assists for 20 points in 18 games, a postseason record. Another one of the good guys in franchise history, Maloney played 11 years, through 1988–1989, and later was an assistant general manager. He ranks fourth on the Rangers' all-time playoff scoring list with 57 points, is tied for seventh with 22 goals, and places third with 35 assists. He is 11th with 502 points, 12th with 195 goals, and 11th with 307 assists. He later became an assistant general manager. Maloney scored 20 goals or more in his first five full seasons and was an All-Star in 1983 and 1984.

Mark Messier

Leadership cannot be taught; it is carried in the marrow and emerges in various ways. Through example. Through demands. Through encouraging patter or stony glare. Through confidence. Through sheer force of will. Through winning. Messier did it all, from Edmonton—the center's hometown and where he would be part of five Cup winners—to New York, a city that had seen his type before: Mickey Mantle, Reggie Jackson, Willis Reed, Lawrence Taylor. But none vanquished a half-century of frustration, in this case during a two-week run in June 1994. Less than three years after he was acquired by general manager Neil Smith, he delivered. After setting franchise records for wins and points during the season, the Rangers were losing to the Devils three games to two in the Eastern Conference Finals. Then came "the Guarantee," followed by a hat trick in Game 6 in New Jersey. After Game 7 of the Finals, he lifted the Cup at the Garden, and a franchise was reborn. No. 11. The Messiah. Moose. Mess. The Captain. In this case, the numbers don't tell the story.

Jean Ratelle

It took 34 years and the greatest player in Czech history to break one of this graceful playmaker's many records: Jaromir Jagr passed 109 points in 2005–2006. That simple fact underscores the importance and the greatness of the franchise's best center. Over 17 years, Ratelle scored 336 goals (second all-time) and 481 assists (third all-time) for 817 points (also third). Starting with Rod Gilbert on the Rangers' junior team in Guelph, Ontario, in 1958, Ratelle was a difference-maker until he was traded in 1975. The linchpin of the Rangers' amazing G-A-G (Goal-a-Game) Line with Gilbert and Vic Hadfield, Ratelle was cool, consistent, and often magnificent. From 1972 to 1976, Ratelle—with 151 goals and 210 assists—had 361 points in 298 games. Only a broken ankle (from a Dale Rolfe shot), which cost him the final 15 games of the season, prevented him from winning the scoring title in 1971–1972. The gifted Quebec native was inducted into the Hockey Hall of Fame in 1985.

Walt Tkaczuk

At first, it was "Tay-chuck." Then it was corrected to "Ka-chook." However his name was pronounced, it meant tenacity and value. Although highly touted as a youngster, Tkaczuk never reached superstardom. But in 13 seasons in New York, the native of Enstedetten, Germany, who grew up in Canada, was a significant contributor, and when his Rangers career was ended by an eye injury at age 33, the stats were formidable: 945 games played, (fifth all-time), 678 points (sixth), 227 goals (11th), and 451 assists (fifth). Centering both Bulldog Lines, Tkaczuk led the team in scoring in his first two full seasons, then morphed into a tough, two-way center. In the 1972 Finals, he shadowed and banged and held the Bruins' Phil Esposito without a goal in six games. Along with Bill Fairbairn, the tandem was one of the league's top penalty-killing units. His early-career scoring should not be over-looked, however: five consecutive 20-goal seasons from 1969–1970 to 1973–1974 and seven goals in 10 playoff games in 1973.

Steve Vickers

Like scientists in a lab, coaches incessantly tweak and twiddle lines to find the right formula. For Vickers, that process worked out swell. Although he was named rookie of the year with 30 goals and 23 assists in the 1971–1972 season, he wasn't a fixture on the line with Walt Tkaczuk and Billy Fairbairn until a month into the season and 16 left wings has been tried and discarded. On November 12, 1972, against Los Angeles, the sparks flew. Vickers scored three goals and added three more in Philadelphia three nights later, the first player in the NHL to post back-to-back hat tricks. The numbers continued to pile up. Vickers, nicknamed "Sarge" because he wore an old green army shirt to practices, played 698 games for New York and registered 246 goals, eighth highest of all time, and 340 assists, good for number nine on the list. Included in his legacy: in his first four seasons, he scored 30 or more goals and a career-high 41 in 1974–1975. And on February 18, 1976, he set a team mark with seven points (three goals and four assists) against Washington.

DEFENSE

Ron Greschner

When Greschner retired in 1990 after 16 seasons, he held the Rangers' records for goals, points, and assists for a defenseman. They were all usurped by Brian Leetch, but that should not over-shadow Greschner's mighty contributions after he was drafted in the second round in 1974. Before his back problems became an issue, Greschner sometimes was used as a forward to maximize his capabilities. A smooth skater and stickhandler, the 6'2" Greschner set a record for rookie assists with 37, and in 1981 scored a career-best 27 goals while sliding in on left wing with the outstanding Swedish stars Anders Hedberg and Ulf Nilsson. The next two seasons were washouts due to back problems. The Saskatchewan native—who found a second home in Manhattan—soldiered on, finishing with 982 games played, fourth all-time behind Harry Howell, Rod Gilbert, and Brian Leetch. With 610 points on 179 goals and 431 assists, Greschner ranks seventh on the all-time scoring list and is the second-highest scoring defenseman behind Leetch.

Harry Howell

Most games by a Rangers defenseman, 1160. Fifth in points, 345. Sixth in goals, 82. For 17 seasons, from 1952–1953 to 1968–1969, Howell was Mr. Reliable. He joined the Rangers at age 19 after one game in the minors and scored a goal in his first game, a backhan-der from the blueline that went over the shoulder of goalkeeper Harry Lumley in Toronto. He never went back to the minors again. In 1966–1967, when he won the Norris Trophy, he said that he was pleased because "that guy in Boston is going to win it for the next 10 years." Close. Bobby Orr would own it until 1976, when Denis Potvin was named top defenseman. Nonetheless, Howell was a mainstay in the down years for the club and was the first Ranger to be honored by a night—January 25, 1967—during which he received a car. A bad back that prompted spinal fusion surgery that summer ended his Rangers career, but he talked GM Emile Francis into a transaction. The Hamilton, Ontario, native was sold to the California Seals, and he completed his NHL career with the Los Angeles Kings in 1972–1973. Like the Energizer Bunny, Howell kept moving. He then spent three years with the World Hockey Association before retiring.

Ching Johnson

The Rangers' first enforcer, Johnson was a burly, hard-hitting defenseman who anchored the blue line on the Cup-winning teams of 1927–1928 and 1932–1933. In 403 games over 11 years, he had 798 penalty minutes (he led the team in that category for seven of those years) and was elected to the Hall of Fame in 1958. His specialty was a solo, down-the-middle rush. Ivan Wilfred Johnson, known as "Ching"—a nickname that stuck when he cooked for pals on offseason hunting and fishing trips, a duty reserved for a man of Asian descent—was an original Ranger recruited by Conn Smythe at age 28. Loved by the fans in the galleries at the first Garden, the popular Johnson retired but came back for one season with the rival New York Americans. His old fans presented him with a gold watch at center ice before his first game. He went on to play around the U.S. and Canada until he was 46. A five-time All-Star, Johnson was elected to the Hall of Fame in 1958.

Brian Leetch

The Rangers' most prolific defenseman and arguably the greatest U.S.-born defenseman, Leetch holds team records for overall assists by a defenseman (741), points by a defenseman (981), and goals by a defenseman (240). A superb power-play quarterback who spent 17 years with the club, the Texas-born, but Connecticut-raised Leetch started his Rangers career by winning rookie of the year in his first full campaign, the 1987–1988 season. He played in three Olympics for Team USA, the first in 1988 after one year at Boston College. The low-key, 11-time All-Star went on to win the Norris Trophy twice, in 1991–1992—only the fifth d-man to top 100 points with 102—and again in 1996–1997. It was his postseason performance in the 1993–1994 Cup season that resonates, however. Leetch registered 11 goals and 23 assists in 23 games to become the only American to win the Conn Smythe Trophy as the postseason MVP. To both Leetch and Rangers fans, who wanted to see him end his career as a Ranger, his trade to Toronto on March 3, 2004, remains a major disappointment. At 38, Leetch officially ended his 18-year NHL career in May 2007 and watched his No. 2 jersey soar to the Garden rafters on January 24, 2008, the fifth such sweater to be retired.

James Patrick

Look up "two-way defenseman" in a dictionary and you might see a picture of James Patrick. "Bittersweet ending" might fit the bill as well. After almost 10 years as a stabilizing force on the Rangers' blue line, Patrick just missed out on a Stanley Cup in the 1993–1994 season, when he was traded early that year with Darren Turcotte to Hartford for Steve Larmer, Nick Kypreos, and others. Patrick, the ninth overall selection in the 1981 NHL Draft, joined the Rangers after skating for the Canadian National Team at the 1984 Winter Olympics in Sarajevo. For the next 10 years, Patrick accumulated some special numbers: he ended his Rangers career with 104 goals, 363 assists, and 467 points, all third in those categories for a defenseman. The 363 assists are eighth overall for any Ranger. In 1991–1992 the Winnipeg native known as "Jeep" scored 14 goals and added 57 assists for 71 points, posting career highs in points, assists, and games played (80). None of his goals, however, were as clutch as the one in the last game of the 1985–1986 season with 16 seconds left against the Capitals that clinched a playoff berth.

Brad Park

One player stood above Douglas Bradford Park as the top defenseman of the late 1960s and early 1970s: Bobby Orr. Park, a Massachusetts native who would have a tremendous career with the Bruins after seven glorious seasons with the Rangers, was the Rangers' first draft pick (1966) to ever make the big club, which he accomplished in 1968. Park, who wore No. 2, was both prickly and prolific. He was the first Rangers defenseman to score a hat trick, on December 12, 1971, and maintains the only scoring

Former New York Rangers (from front to back) Mark Messier, Mike Richter, Ed Giacomin, and Rod Gilbert listen to the speech by Brian Leetch (not pictured) during Leetch's jersey retirement ceremony in January 2008. Leetch joins these four players as the only Rangers to have their numbers retired. Photo courtesy of Getty Images.

record by a defenseman not held by Brian Leetch or Ron Greschner: 25 goals in the 1973–1974 season, when he led the team in scoring with 87 points. His 95 goals rank fifth as a Rangers d-man, and 283 assists and 378 points are both fourth on the all-time list for Rangers blueliners. He captained the team until the blockbuster trade in November 1975 that included four stars: Park and Jean Ratelle went to Boston for Phil Esposito and Carol Vadnais. In 17 years, his NHL teams never missed the playoffs.

GOALTENDERS

Ed Giacomin

Neither of his two dreams—to score a goal and win a Stanley Cup—ever materialized. But the lanky Giacomin reined in the Rangers' crease for 10 years, beginning in 1965–1966. He is second on the franchise's career victory list (267), had 49 shutouts in 539 games, and shared the Vezina Trophy in 1971 with Gilles Villemure. In 1965–1966 the Rangers had not been in the playoffs for four years, and Giacomin helped end that skein. The Cup dream died in 1972, when the Rangers lost to Bobby Orr and Boston. Giacomin was one of the first few netminders to wander from the crease, going behind the net to trap the puck like Jacques Plante. He led NHL goaltenders in wins (30), games played (68), and shutouts (nine), and began a series of playoff runs that would last a decade. Only in 1975–1976, when he was waived and later claimed by the Red Wings on Halloween, did the postseason streak end. Although his skills had deteriorated at age 36, when he beat the Rangers in an emotional return to the Garden a few days after the Wings picked him up, he was welcomed back as a hero.

Dave Kerr

In March 1938 Kerr was hockey's cover boy, appearing on the front of *Time* magazine: "While the goal-scoring forward line goes zooming towards fame and the two burly defensemen crash violently against their opponents to the cheers of the galleries," the article about the game read, "the goaltender, encased in 25 lb. of pads, is grimly occupied with the job of making saves." At that time, Kerr was in the midst of a five-year run in which he was the only man to start in the Rangers' net. The Toronto native backstopped the team to the 1937 Finals and then capped it off by helping the Rangers win the 1940 Stanley Cup in six games over his hometown Maple Leafs. Kerr missed only one game between 1934 and 1941. During the 1939–1940 season, when he played all 48 games, Kerr had a 19-game unbeaten streak (14–0–5) and captured the Vezina Trophy. Kerr's career numbers were sensational. From 1934–1935 to 1940–1941, he won 157 games, lost 110, and tied 57, with a magnificent 2.07 goals-against average, an eye-popping 40 shutouts, and a postseason goals-against average of 1.57 in 33 games.

Mike Richter

"The Save." For a guy who loves to talk, those two words are his contribution to the Rangers' lexicon. In Game 4 of the 1994 Stanley Cup Finals in Vancouver, the acrobatic Richter stopped Pavel Bure on a penalty shot with his right pad at the goal post to change the fortunes of the series and help the Rangers win their first Cup in 54 years. Perhaps the greatest U.S.-born goaltender, Richter, who wore a Statue of Liberty mask, is the team's career leader in victories (301) and appearances by a goaltender (666). In 1994 Richter set franchise records for playoff wins (16) and most shutouts in a playoff run (four). The Abington, Pennsylvania, native was a three-time All-Star who posted 24 shutouts and a 2.68 goals-against average in a career that began in 1989 and ended in 2003, after sustaining a fractured skull from a slap shot and a concussion eight months later. A second-round draft pick, Richter became not only a New York hockey legend, but a world-class goaltender. He backstopped the United States team that won the World Cup in 1996 and the silver medal in the Salt Lake City Olympics in 2002.

Gump Worsley

Think of this number: 34,675. That's how many minutes Lorne "Gump" Worsley tended goal for the Rangers, mostly as a short, stocky, but agile target on a series of defenseless Rangers teams. In 1952–1953 Worsley, who grew up in Montreal, stepped in for an injured Chuck Rayner and won the rookie of the year award at 23. He is the only Rangers goaltender to do so. Worsley, a stand-up style netminder who refused to wear a mask when many colleagues were protecting themselves, received more than 200 stitches in his face over the years, while facing between 30 and 40 shots a night. But he survived and flourished, only not in the shooting gallery of Madison Square Garden. After a decade in New York, compiling a record of 204–269–101 in 582 games, Worsley was traded to the Canadiens, who were far more defensive-minded. He shared two Vezina Trophies in Montreal, was on four Cup-winning teams, and was elected to the Hall of Fame in 1980.

RESERVES

Camille Henry

On November 1, 1959, when the look of hockey changed, "the Eel" was part of it. Montreal's Jacques Plante donned a mask that night, and Cammy Henry scored the only goal against him. The elusive center/left wing—who was the smallest player in the NHL in the late 1950s—would score 255 more as a Ranger. The Quebec City native was rookie of the year in 1954—edging the great Jean Beliveau—won the Lady Byng Memorial Trophy in 1958 and was captain in the 1964–1965 season. In his freshman year, he scored four goals in a March 13 game against Detroit's Terry Sawchuk, the only time that occurred. Because of his size (5'7"), Henry was often injured and wore knee braces. When Emile Francis became general manager in 1965, he shipped the popular Henry to Chicago for Doug Robinson, John Brenneman, and Wayne Hillman, but reacquired him in early 1968. In 637 games over 12 years, Henry had 476 points, putting him 12th all-time in franchise history and just 78 penalty minutes, the second fewest of any Ranger in the top 30 in team scoring, behind Andy Hebenton (75) who played in 77 fewer games.

Andy Hebenton

If you were a Rangers fan in the late 1950s and early 1960s, you couldn't miss Andy Hebenton. The right winger from Winnipeg played every game. He played 560 consecutive games for the Rangers, plus 22 more in the Stanley Cup playoffs, and the 582-game streak is the Rangers' all-time record. When he was claimed by Boston, he didn't miss a game in the 1964–1965 season, and the 630 consecutive regular-season games made him the Cal Ripken Jr. of his era. He was more than just durable, though. In those days, the hustling Hebenton played on the second line with Camille Henry and Red Sullivan, and averaged more than 20 goals a season. Because he also killed penalties, the dutiful Ontario native was known as "Handy Andy." Sullivan described him to Rangers historian John Halligan as "the perfect team player. He didn't say a whole lot, but he led by example."

Dave Maloney

A passionate, competitive player on the ice—and later on Wall Street and in the broadcast booth—Maloney was the youngest captain in Rangers history and youngest captain among all NHL teams in 1978–1979, just two months after his 22nd birthday. He and younger brother Don were the only brother combination selected by the team in the first round; Dave was 14th, Don was 20th. In his 11 years on Broadway, Maloney rose above a litany of injuries (broken leg in 1976, severed left arm tendon in 1977, torn knee ligaments in 1978 and 1981) to finish his New York career with 70 goals (seventh all-time among defensemen), 225 assists (also seventh), 295 points (eighth), and 1,115 penalty minutes (fourth all-time). Off the ice, Maloney was one of the most literate Rangers; he read newspapers, books, and pored over crossword puzzles. Maloney was traded along with Chris Renaud to Buffalo for Steve Patrick and Jim Wiemer on December 6, 1984.

COACHES

Emile Francis

The former backup goaltender known as "the Cat," Francis rebuilt a staggering franchise that had made the playoffs only once in the previous eight seasons and then played in the postseason for nine straight, including the Finals in 1971–1972. As coach and general manager beginning in December 1965, the Rangers initially finished in last place with an 18–41–11 record. Then came the turnaround. In 1966–1967 Harry Howell, then 34, won the Norris Trophy, and Boom Boom Geoffrion, arriving from Montreal, spurred the Rangers to a 15–4–3 run and a postseason berth. From then one, Francis's mantra was: youth, depth, and size ruled. He drafted Brad Park, Walt Tkaczuk, and Ron Greschner. He acquired Ed Giacomin from Providence. The G-A-G and Bulldog Lines flourished in his era, which saw the league expand from six to 12 teams, and the Rangers moved to the current Madison Square Garden. Francis leads all Rangers coaches with 654 games, 342 wins, and a .602 winning percentage. Although the Rangers didn't win a Stanley Cup on his watch, the renaissance provided a blueprint for years to come.

Lester Patrick

One of the sons of a millionaire Western Canada lumberman, Patrick played all seven positions during his early hockey career, including rover, a midfield-type position after the turn of the century. After founding the Pacific Coast Hockey Association—and playing defense—Patrick was tabbed as coach of the expansion Rangers in 1926 as a last-minute replacement for Conn Smythe. His knowledge of the Canadian leagues and players helped greatly, as the Rangers won two Stanley Cup championships in their first seven years. Patrick, who had played just one NHL game when he inserted himself into the lineup as a defenseman when the team was battling injuries during the 1926–1927 season, achieved cult status in New York at age 44. He came out from behind the bench to play goal for the Rangers during the last 46 minutes of Game 2 of the Stanley Cup Finals in 1928 after Lorne Chabot was injured. Patrick allowed just one goal and got the win when Frank Boucher scored in overtime. "The Silver Fox" coached 604 games, had 281 wins, and a .554 winning percentage, all second only to Emile Francis. The Lester Patrick Awards are given annually for outstanding service to hockey in the United States.

Honorable Mentions

Roger Neilson (141 wins), Herb Brooks (131 wins), and Mike Keenan (52 in 1994, the Cup year). And Tom Renney may pass both Francis and Patrick. Or the wheel may turn again. After all, nothing lasts forever when it comes to the Rangers.